Culture and Anarchism

By the same author
People Without Government: an anthropology of anarchy

FREEDOM PRESS publish *Freedom* (fortnightly) and *The Raven* (quarterly) as well as books (more than sixty titles in print).

FREEDOM PRESS BOOKSHOP carries the most comprehensive stock of anarchist literature, including titles from North America. Please send for our current list.

Freedom Press
in Angel Alley
84b Whitechapel High Street
London
E1 7QX

Culture
and
Anarchism

Harold Barclay

FREEDOM PRESS
London

Published by
FREEDOM PRESS
84b Whitechapel High Street
London E1 7QX
1997

ISBN 0 900384 84 0

Typeset by Jayne Clementson
Printed in Great Britain by Aldgate Press, London E1

Contents

Introduction

I am pleased to accept the invitation of Freedom Press to offer here some of my writings which may be of special interest to anarchists and other libertarians. Much of what I have written has been in the area of my specialisation in the contemporary peoples of Egypt and the northern Sudan (see, for example, *Buurri al Lamaab: A Suburban Village in the Sudan*, 1964). Religion has also been a focus of mine, but there is little of this in this book because most of my research in this field addresses specific issues in Islamic studies and, like the ethnographic work on Egypt and the Sudan, would not be appropriate in this context. Articles on religion of more general interest have been recently published in *The Raven* (No. 27, 1994) and need not therefore be reissued here. These include 'The Roman Catholic Church: The Unholy Trinity of Tiger, Fox and Lamb' and 'The Protestant Tradition, the Moral Majority and Freedom'.

Except for two articles, all the essays in this book have been previously published. Regarding the 'Comment on John Zerzan's Critique of Agriculture', I was asked by *Fifth Estate* in 1988 for my reaction to an article by Zerzan advocating the abolition of agriculture. However, because my remarks somehow did not conform to the *Fifth Estate* party line, it was not published. I therefore offer it here. 'Of People and Chimps' was an essay I wrote after reading Dudley Young's *Origins of the Sacred*.

I have hesitated about including book reviews in this collection, but I believe that those that have been included help to explicate my views of the free and humane society. In general, I have tried here to present the materials in such a fashion that they reflect some more or less coherent theoretical orientation as well as an overall view of my idea of anarchism.

The book is divided into three sections. In the first I consider the concept of culture which has always been central to my view of human nature and behaviour. Two points are worthy of emphasis here. First, it seems to me that the mind is a structure which organises and categorises external reality. At the same time with humans, the mind is saturated by a learned culture which further imposes a structure through which external stimuli are arranged and organised. Thus, the world in a sense becomes my idea. Furthermore, whatever reality exists out there is not purely material, that is, not merely individual

atoms or particles (assuming they are, in fact, 'material'), but also –
equally important, if not more so – is the non-material organisation
or configuration of those particles. My view is then not a materialist
one, but is what some choose to call mentalist, drawing upon Kant
and Cassirer among others. In this way my notions may diverge from
those of many anarchists. The second point I would emphasise is that
mono-causal explanations of human behaviour are simplistic and
erroneous. I deal briefly with a number of these – interestingly
enough, materialistic – theories in the chapter on 'Cultural
Dynamics'. I have thought it worthwhile to include these chapters
from my book *Culture, the Human Way*, particularly since it is no
longer in print. Readers may also wish to refer to my article in *The
Raven* (No. 18, 1992) 'Anarchism and Anthropology'.

Another major segment in this section is the concluding chapter
from *People Without Government: An Anthropology of Anarchy*. Much
of this summarises characteristics of the numerous types of anarchic
polities which have existed in the past. It also considers the origins of
the state and the future possibilities of anarchy. Nicolas Walter, in a
review of *People Without Government* which appeared in both the *New
Statesman* and *Freedom*, wrote: "Barclay's book, published by a small
general publisher and a smaller anarchist publisher, has been
excellently edited and despite beginning as a clumsy and confused
manuscript now reads clearly and elegantly." I don't know where
Walter got this idea, but it is rubbish. Not a word of the original
manuscript was ever changed by any editors. The original, unaltered
manuscript became the book.

A short second section of this volume contains pieces which deal
with social movements, and especially 'utopian' communities.
Regarding the latter, I believe that the more successful of such
experiments may be those which are not radical deviations from
traditional culture and include a membership with strong dedication
to the notion of individual responsibility. Hopefully they might also
be loosely organised and highly flexible, although it is to be noted that
the most successful intentional community movement has been the
Hutterites who are strongly patriarchal and rigidly organised.

A final group of essays concerns specific problems in anarchist
theory. Here I would suggest, among other things, that many
anarchist theoreticians have not always been very consistently
anarchist, and I use Proudhon and Warren as examples, even though

they remain my two favourite anarchist theoreticians. Some idea of what I think an anarchist society would be like is offered in the short piece on 'Anarchism and Cities'.

I have not written to any extent on environmental and related issues. This does not mean that I have no interest in such problems. Rather, I have concentrated on writing on those topics with which I am most thoroughly familiar. I have also tried to follow the policy of not engaging in the repetition of what others have already written, especially when they would say it better. This environmental or ecological area has now become of central importance in anarchist and other circles. At the same time certain ideas on the subject have apparently become widely accepted and yet largely unrefuted. I would like, therefore, to take this opportunity to make two or three points about them, specifically concerning 'specieism', a direction in evolution and mutual aid as a factor in evolution.

I suppose I am what would be referred to as a specieist. I believe that my first obligation is to my fellow humans. As I would prefer my son and daughter to others more distantly or not related to me, so also I would give priority to fellow humans over non-humans. I cannot see how a cockroach or a mosquito can be as worthy as a human being. This does not mean that I endorse a callous attitude to other forms of life or that I accept the Old Testament view of the Earth being given by God to humankind to dominate and exploit. I accept Albert Schweitzer's doctrine of reverence for life and the view that humans can act as stewards of the Earth's resources and the variety of life upon it. Such a view can probably best be explained by the examples of hunting wild game and the care of domesticated animals. Reverence for life prohibits hunting wild game as sport, but it is conceivable when necessary for the preservation of human individuals. Occasional culling of wild game is sometimes required as well to ward off deadly epidemics. Deer, for instance, when overpopulated largely through lack of natural predators, can develop parasitic epidemics. For domesticated animals reverence for life would lead to opposition to many practices in contemporary Western agriculture, such as battery production of poultry, methods of producing white veal and the crating of sows giving birth. No animal needs to be pumped full of antibiotics and drugs to enhance performance. Animals may also be trained; they don't need to be 'broken'.

I cannot agree with those who would argue that the evolutionary process has any kind of direction, particularly towards something called progress. It seems to me that the evolutionary process as a natural process cannot have direction. To suggest teleology of any kind is to suggest that there is a mind of some sort guiding the whole operation. And a process cannot have a mind. It is true that evolution demonstrates certain patterns: there is bilateral symmetry; that there are a very few phyla and classes of living forms indicates a limited number of basic patterns. And in evolution more complex forms have ordinarily appeared after simpler forms. But this does not mean direction. If, for example, the movement from simple to complex indicated a direction the more complex would replace the simpler. But such is not the case. The simplest organisms exist alongside the most complex, and the most successful forms in terms of longevity on this earth and in numbers of organisms have been the simpler forms, e.g. bacteria and insects, which continually threaten the survival of the most complex: the mammals and the birds. Paraphrasing a well known statement: God's favourite form of life must have been the beetle, since there are tens of thousands of species of beetles. On the other hand, ants may be the favourite since they constitute almost one-third of the total animal biomass. The belief in direction in nature, especially of one towards progress, arises from an anthropocentric view of the world with humans as the capping stone of all 'creation'.

The evolutionary process operates on the principle of species and individual preservation. Species not only survive by mutual aid and cooperation, but also by competition and violence. All are important mechanisms of evolution. Mutual aid is clearly not the main factor since there is no main factor. As Kropotkin said, mutual aid is *a* factor in evolution. As the television nature shows have erroneously over-stressed the blood and gore, the competition and violence of wild life, so others have erroneously ignored these as part of the story and have over-stressed mutual aid.

Is there an ethic within the evolutionary process? Some suggest it is mutual aid, but I have tried here to indicate that the situation is entirely too ambiguous to make such an assertion. Rather, I would offer a more modified view. Evolution, itself, has no morality, but humans can extract from it ideas which can form the basis for a moral system. We can look back at the history of humans, specifically, and extrapolate from this the broad hint of an ethic. We may note that reciprocity and mutual aid have been apparent universally in human society, but that for most humans this has meant a mutual aid that is applicable to the local group and is not universal. As near as can be determined, archaic humans had no generalised conception of humanity, meaning all humankind. Their sense of obligation was to others within the small neighbourhood group of kin and close friends. Those who believe that archaic humans as hunter-gatherers lived in a loving harmony with each other and with nature have not familiarised themselves with the archaeological and ethnographic record, the only records we have which can tell anything about how our ancestors lived.

Feuding and conflict go back to the earliest days of humanity. And the idea that indigenous or archaic peoples were somehow more in tune with nature and less destructive and callous about it is controversial to say the least. It may be true that they were less destructive because they understood more about conservation, but there were also very few of them and they lacked adequate tools and weapons for that destruction. Even so, there is a strong suspicion that the small population of North America ten thousand years ago with their limited weaponry made a major contribution to the extermination of several species of large herbivores in this continent.

Ideas about mutual aid and cooperation in earliest antiquity were part of the practice associated with the local group and seen as primarily applicable to it alone. In the course of time such ideas became more generalised as applicable to larger groups, such as the early states in Mesopotamia and Egypt. The so-called Axial Age (during the first millennium BCE) appears as a period in which, from numerous independent locations in the world, there developed the idea of a universally applicable morality. The old notion of mutual aid within the local group was generalised to advocate mutual aid, cooperation and respect for all humans. It is no accident that most of the so-called Great Religions which teach the Golden Rule and appeared in such disparate locations as Palestine, Iran, India and China, should arise at this time. It was a period of increasing population, increasing differentiation in the division of labour, increasing variety in the community, increasing urbanisation, and the appearance of empire. Thus socio-cultural circumstances of the day provoked such development. As societies came to incorporate large and more heterogeneous populations in often intimate living arrangements, the applicability of the mutual aid idea became more broadly relevant and appropriate to harmonious living.

In sum, a universal ethic of mutual aid has emerged in the course of the historical development of our species and it emerged and became widely accepted because people saw that life is enhanced when they worked together and engaged in reciprocal aid. The problem, of course, is that while this idea emerges, the other practices of competition and violence persist and institutions such as the state, empire and capitalism arise which reinforce violence and mayhem. The Great Religions become captives of a state so that none ever have been successful in spreading the *practice* of a universal morality.

Ironically, we humans have experienced an enormous increase in our knowledge and understanding of the world, but at the same time our violent and malignant social relations and destructive exploitation of the earth do not change. We seem hardly closer to a community of freedom, peace and abundance for all. Thus I would emphasise what I concluded in the last few lines of *People Without Government*, namely, a truly free society may never be attained, but that is no reason to abandon the struggle, for to do so is to abandon life.

CULTURE:
AN ANTHROPOLOGICAL
AND ANARCHIST PERSPECTIVE

1.

Culture: The Unifying Concept of Anthropology

Basic characteristics

North American anthropology has traditionally organised its principal subject matter – the behaviour, history and diversity of human beings – around a central unifying concept of culture. However, there has never been consensus concerning the precise meaning of the term. In addition, culture is a word, like many in the social sciences, which has been employed in a variety of ways outside the field of anthropology and indeed it was lifted by anthropologists from the realm of general usage.

Despite several interpretations within and outside anthropology, there is nevertheless a common core of shared significance and meaning attached to the word. That is, culture suggests something which is developed, refined, domesticated or cultivated. In one widely held view culture is the music of Bach or Beethoven, but clearly not rock and roll; it is the works of Shakespeare or Tolstoy, but not the Mutt and Jeff comic strip; it is fine French wine, but not Manneshevits. In all cases the distinction is one of the presumably refined and cultivated versus the crude, the 'natural', and uncultivated. That which is cultural should not be confused with the natural, the rude or the wild. Or, as Levi-Strauss writes, culture is the cooked, nature is the raw. Horti-culture and agri-culture entail the planting of a limited number of domesticated plants in some order and continually nurturing them, particularly keeping out the 'weeds'. By contrast, in nature there are no weeds.

In anthropological usage rock and roll, Mutt and Jeff and Manneshevits are just as much cultural as Beethoven or Shakespeare, but still to every anthropologist the cultural is that which is modified, refined, cultivated or domesticated in accord with some notions in what is ordinarily a human 'mind'.

Kluckhohn and Kelly defined culture as "All those historically created designs for living, explicit and implicit, rational, irrational and non-rational, which exist at any given time as potential guides for the behaviour of men" (1945, 97). Culture is learned or acquired 'ideas' – beliefs, knowledge, plans for action, rules and understandings – that are available to a people in a given society.

Thus for the anthropologist what is cultural includes a vast number of different things – all of which have in common the fact that they are learned and for the most part invented. That a broad umbrella-like concept such as culture should be the most central concept in anthropology reflects the distinctive 'holistic' nature of anthropology. Culture is a holistic concept encompassing most everything that people think about.

It is necessary to clarify this concept somewhat further and to address several complex and perplexing issues: first is the locus of culture; second is the shared nature of culture; third is whether culture is exclusively human. Fourth, we may consider the extent to which culture may be 'reality' or a mere construct.

The locus of culture
Differences amongst anthropologists concerning where culture may be located and the nature of its ultimate reality arise out of opposing philosophical positions, often reduced to a contrast between materialists and idealists, also sometimes disparagingly referred to as mentalists.

Traditional materialism holds that reality is ultimately composed of isolated indivisible particles or 'atoms' which have the quality of extension in space and duration in time. In anthropological theory this philosophy is expressed in views which find the reality of culture, that is, the fundamental causal or moving force in culture, in two main areas: 1) in the material objects of human manufacture – the physical tools employed, and 2) the observed behaviour of humans and particularly in those social institutions which are directly concerned with production and distribution of material goods. This refers especially to the economy. Some materialists would emphasise extra cultural, but nonetheless material phenomena, such as population dynamics, genetics and physical environment.

Critics of materialism suggest that it was more amenable to a nineteenth century notion of physics, but modern science has, especially in quantum theory, upset much scientific certainty in regard to physical laws, the nature of mechanics and matter. The latter may be seen as particles at one moment and waves at another. Some would say that the important characteristics of matter as extension in space and duration in time seem to evaporate into a sequence of forms or events.

Even if we grant the reality of some kind of atoms or particles in the traditional materialist manner, we must note that these particles have distinct relationships to one another. They possess a structure or comprise a configuration of a relatively stable relationship to one another. Such stable patterns are non-material features which are clearly as much a part of an 'ultimate reality' as the particles themselves. Reality is not a congeries of atomic particles. The non-material features of organisation or configuration and therefore the laws of nature themselves are just as much a part of reality as the particles themselves. Indeed, as seems to be advocated by some observers of the natural world, it is possibly the relationships which are the important and fundamental entities. The materialist may point to the stone blocks as the ultimate units in a great cathedral; but the mentalist or idealist suggests that these blocks must be arranged in a specific design and that this is what creates the cathedral. Thus, organisation and pattern are paramount.

One mentalist or idealist view in addition stresses that all any human knows about the world around him is processed through the brain or mind, an instrument which organises and categorises the world. Principles of organisation and categorisation of the world may be inherent in the general nature of the brain of *Homo sapiens*. This parallels a point of view elaborated by Immanuel Kant and one also explored by the linguist Noam Chomsky, and by the anthropologist Claude Levi-Strauss. Additional principles of organisation are cultural. They are acquired, beginning with the moment of birth, so that by the time a child is only a few years old he has had inculcated within him patterns of outlook, points of view and ways of ordering external reality which he believes are perfectly 'natural' and are in a way an integral part of his person. Further, according to the psychologist Piaget the individual himself is actively involved in this organising process. The idealist argues that any human has a mental system which interacts with and organises the external environment. Contrary to Locke the human mind or brain does not commence as a *tabula rasa* and certainly very early in life it has become an active force in creating reality for the individual.

This is to say therefore that we see and act in relationship to a world of appearances. What we know comes to us in the form of ideas. Our reality, our world, is therefore one of ideas. Whether or not one can ever know some kind of ultimate reality, things as they 'really' are, is a question. Presumably some scientists would argue that scientific laws are breakthroughs to this ultimate reality. On the other hand, Kant, for example, argued that such laws are constructs of the human mind. They are our idea of the world. Thus, we must remain sceptical of the materialist argument that ultimate reality is some kind of indivisible particle and that all ideas are reducible to matter for above all the only things we know directly are ideas; we only know matter indirectly through our idea of it. Also, equally untenable is that extreme idealist position which holds that only ideas exist. Finally, many have deprecated the old arguments between materialists and idealists as unproductive and a peculiar obsession of Western minds. As particles may become waves and waves become particles so also 'matter' and 'idea' may be only aspects of the same ultimate reality. And if this underlying reality has different faces, perhaps then there are different realities. Ultimate reality becomes a figment.

In the latter part of this essay there is an extended discussion of various materialist conceptions of cultural causation and change. Here I wish to explore further the materialist definition of culture as behaviour and its material products as against the mentalist's emphasis upon ideas.

If we accept that culture is 'ideas' and that the ultimate locus of these ideas is in people's heads (*cf.* Goodenough) we encounter a number of problems which are clearly avoided by a materialist orientation. The mentalist may be charged with mysticism. At least these 'ideas' are not readily captured by scientific procedures. We have an additional problem of how this notion can be reconciled with another common feature of things cultural – their shared nature – an issue we shall consider in a moment.

To say that culture's ultimate locus is within people's heads further raises the issue as to whether stored information can be part of culture. Even amongst a people who have no tradition of writing various mnemonic devices are employed. Pictures and designs and other technological devices also may be used to store information. In modern society with libraries of millions of volumes, with thousands of periodicals, films, recording devices and elaborate computers, one could say that most of the 'ideas' in our culture are not stored in human brains but in products of human brains. However, the point is that to become effective in the human community all this stored material must pass into and through human brains. Neither the book nor the computer program have any significance unless they are read by a person. So from this point of view it is still valid to put the ultimate locus of culture in the human head.

If we consider culture to be behaviour and its products then the question immediately arises why human behaviour is so highly variant and so complex while other animal behaviour is so uniform within a given species and so ubiquitously simple. Asking this question leads us to individuals and the activity which goes on in their brains, namely among *Homo sapiens* we observe that this behaviour is almost entirely acquired – it is learned from others. That of animals is almost entirely a product of genetic programming – of instinct. If we ask another question about culture as behaviour, such as what motivates it, we get back to considering the same problem. That is, back to what goes on inside people's heads. Merely defining culture as behaviour and its products does not get to the fundamental difference between kinds of behaviour: those that are learned in a social context and those which are instinctive or a product of body chemistry. To do this we must, so to speak, go behind the behaviour and material manifestations of behaviour. We may then consider that culture, as is suggested by the definitions which commence this section, is ideas, plans for action, designs for living which ultimately are inside people's heads.

Culture clearly manifests itself in behaviour and in concrete material objects – objects of these ideas. There is no such thing as material culture, only material manifestations of culture. The typewriter is a manifestation of culture. What is culturally relevant regarding the typewriter is the complex of 'ideas': techniques, conceptions, action plans, which provide the blueprints or recipe for manufacturing such a machine and the technique for its operation. Furthermore, to provide a second example, two individuals encountering one another and proceeding to shake right hands while they exchange a few sounds represents a pattern of behaviour which is not culture but a manifestation of it. Indeed, it is these very manifestations by which an anthropologist, or any person for that matter, derives or infers a 'culture'. People speak; they produce a hammer or some other tool; they perform certain standardised bodily movements we call rituals.

Since the actor is observed to behave or speak in a certain way we infer that this is part of a parcel of ideas that is inside his head and which he has acquired over time.

But the ideas are not produced there by some kind of immaculate conception. We must infer that they are there as a consequence of the interaction of the individual with other individuals and with the non-human environment so that culture in fact results from a dialectic process. From the day of birth each individual is 'brainwashed'. He has the various traditions of his culture inculcated within him so they become second nature. He learns other people's ideas as these are manifested to him through behaviour and manufactured material objects. The individual internalises these objectified entities so that they become fixed as ideas within his own brain. However, each individual will internalise these cultural manifestations in his own way – that is, giving each his peculiar stamp. In a way everyone, therefore, is an innovator in some ordinarily slight fashion. Further, the transmission of this culture varies from family to family. Thus the process of cultural transmission is not one of cloning but one which produces variants of the same theme. The dialectic process is one of continual interaction of the individual with the environment and one therefore in which cultural elements may be seen at one time as so many manifestations imposing themselves on the individual and at another as ideas within the individual.

As was mentioned above, the human mind is not a *tabula rasa*, a blank tablet or empty container which passively receives messages and content from the external environment. Rather the 'mind' constitutes an integrated organising system which selects, categorises and sifts out what it receives and in so doing manipulates, modifies and alters external stimuli. Further, contributory to this manipulating and organising function is the peculiar autobiography of the individual himself and the peculiar culture into which he is being immersed. In other words, when we refer to the individual in the dialectic process we are assuming at least three levels of input: one, the built-in structure of mind, and two other acquired influences: the peculiar autobiography of the individual and the cultural milieu.

The dialectic is an active ongoing interaction between the individual and the outside. It entails culture being constantly invented by the interaction of 'mind' and environment and it is the continual alteration between material manifestations of culture and ideas in people's heads. And paramount in such a process is the social construction of culture – the building of shared meanings through human interaction (*cf.* Geertz, 1973, and also Keesing, 1981, especially 97 ff). This 'mentalist' conception, and one which rejects the notion of a material culture, it is argued here, is a logically more consistent position than that which so defines culture as to include not only the internalised ideas but also the objects of those ideas in external reality. This latter position is one which tends to make of culture a large congeries of totally disparate elements.

The position assumed here concerning the nature of the human mind and stressing the active and creative role of the individual in the making of culture and his own person is one which clearly underscores the ideas of freedom and personal dignity. The alternate view of the mind as a *tabula rasa* implicitly sees humans as so many blank tablets passively accepting whatever some manipulator wishes to engrave upon them (Chomsky, 1975, especially 128 ff).

Culture as shared

It is common to speak of culture in the anthropological sense as not only learned but shared. Such notions are implicit in terms like custom or tradition. They suggest the important process of ideas being passed on with minimum modification from one generation to the next and from one peer to another. Thus individual idiosyncrasies are normally not viewed as part of culture. This 'sharedness' attribute, however, creates a few problems. First, if culture is ideas that are in people's heads, how do they become shared? The anthropological observer can only infer that an idea expressed by one person and the same or similar one expressed by another are therefore indications of sharing.

Secondly, we may ask in what manner are these ideas to be shared; how similar or alike must expressions by two different people be before we can say they share the same idea? As we have suggested, the individual is not a passive receptor but actively creates or invents. In no society are all people 'spittin' images' of one another. From, if you will, a highly nominalistic point of view everyone is different; everyone's ideas are different and discrete because they have each been processed through a discrete mental apparatus contained within an individual organism. From a more general point of view, of course, there are innumerable items which might be seen as being shared.

Thus, if we visit a Libyan village we would find that everyone 'shares' in a common belief in Islam, but we will also find that Islam is not the same for everyone. In a similar vein the anthropologist, after prolonged and intensive exposure to a culture, may observe that there exist pervasive, enduring and widely held principles or 'themes' (see Opler, 1945). Such themes are expressed in various areas of the culture and by numerous individuals; they may not be verbalised at all, but the outside observer formulates them and sees them as of no little significance in understanding the pattern of life. An important theme in the culture of the Libyan village would be one of male superiority. Another might be one of the equality of all those of a given age and sex group.

From the above we may surmise that much alleged cultural sharing is actually the same or similar responses made independently by informants to the anthropologist. In this regard cultural sharing is an analytical construct of the anthropologist and is to be distinguished from the 'real' sharing which arises out of the exchange of information by two or more people in ongoing social interaction.

A third problem with the notion of sharedness as part of culture is the question of how many must share before it is considered a legitimate item of a given culture. Is it two or three, or three million? Here we may find that sometimes a trait which is shared by only a few, or even one which is limited to the behaviour of a single person, may be more important to the culture than one which is shared by thousands. Thus in a given society most everyone may blow his nose in the same fashion, but only one person may know all the complex and crucial rituals related to planting and harvest or to death. Finally, as Ralph Linton pointed out, idiosyncratic behaviour always has the potential of becoming widely shared (1936, 274). It is the pool out of which shared cultural items are drawn.

I believe we may say that culture is ordinarily shared in some fashion. The shared nature of culture becomes apparent particularly when culture is collectively and dialectically constructed in the process of social interaction. But in any case, shared or not, culture consists of those ideas – learned and, for the most part, invented – which are always available to the people of a given group. I shall return to this question of sharedness and culture below in considering intra-cultural variability.

Culture is only too human

In the past four hundred years scientific knowledge has demolished one after another the alleged unique features of our world and species. First, human self importance was diminished when it was demonstrated that the earth was not the centre of the universe, but only a minor planet travelling an orbit around an immense sun. Then humans were further insulted as they were placed as one species among hundreds of thousands, albeit the highest and most advanced. It was soon suggested that not only was man just another animal, but he was just another primate among the apes and monkeys and an evolutionary product out of a now extinct ape-like primate. Within the last century we have been informed by astronomers that not only do we reside on a very minor planet revolving around a sun, but that this sun itself is of minor importance and the solar system to which we belong is located in some obscure corner of an immense galaxy which in fact is itself dwarfed in relation to the size of other galaxies and of the universe as a whole.

Today, as well, we have come to realise that humans are not that fundamentally different from chimpanzees and gorillas. The only significant anatomical characteristic of hominids – the biological family to which humans belong – is bipedalism. This walking upright has necessitated other distinctive modifications such as a specialised foot, larger and more powerful muscles and bones on the hind limbs and a spinal column with a lumbar curve and a skull sitting more directly on top of the column. *Homo sapiens* have practically the same genetic material as do chimpanzees.

Nevertheless, some have argued that humans had some fundamentally, ontologically, unique features which made them different from everything else. It has been argued that our uniqueness, our separation from a mundane world, was still salvaged by the great intellectual gulf which separated humans from other living creatures. Humans were still both quantitatively and qualitatively different from other animals since they alone were all symbol users and makers, tool makers and users, and moral beings. Ostwald defined culture as "that which distinguishes men from animals" (1907, 510). Ernst Cassirer called humans *Homo symbolicus* and argued that an impassable abyss separated them from animals in the symbolic capacity which humans alone possessed.

Unfortunately even this claim to uniqueness is put into question by contemporary investigations in animal behaviour which have further blurred the difference between humans and animals. Chimpanzees, for example, have been taught complex sign systems and can be quite ingenious in their use of computers to convey thoughts. They have even been taught to speak a few simple words. Signalling among other animals and birds has been shown to be much more complex than was previously believed. Birds in one region apparently have a 'dialect' which is different from those of the same species living in another region. They are apparently transmitting learned and shared behaviour – technically that is cultural behaviour. In brief, it is clear that animal behaviour cannot be explained away as purely 'instinctive', nor human behaviour as purely cultural.

However, it may be that some investigators go too far in the direction of removing all differences between humans and other animals. I argue that what is distinctly human may not be the cultural behaviour per se. What is distinctly human is the active innovating role of the individual and the total dependence of the individual upon cultural behaviour. Only humans actually invent truly symbolic systems of communication. Only humans actually create a symbolic world within which they live, perceive the world and are forever captive. Chimpanzees may be taught to learn a few symbols, but they have no motivation to invent a symbolic world, no motivation to give everything a name, and even the symbols they do learn are always very concrete. So far as we now know, it is only humans who can discuss or even conceive of abstractions such as truth or honesty. Chimpanzees don't sit around discussing the concept of justice, of freedom, nor do they manufacture fictitious worlds. Humans invent and populate the world with things which do not exist in 'reality'; they can think of the future and know details of their own personal past and of others as well. They know their finitude and ultimate destiny. The extent to which these achievements are shared with any other animals is questionable.

Humans everywhere comprehend and so deal with the world through the categories of a specific culture. It is not an overstatement to say that without culture there is no human and one may seriously doubt how long any human or human group would survive without culture. Of the few cases of individuals raised in such isolated circumstances that they have acquired no culture it is apparent that these persons, in their behaviour, are not human and they are hardly teachable. Geertz has written: "Like the cabbage it so much resembles, the *Homo* *sapiens'* brain, having arisen within the framework of human culture, would not be viable outside of it". A cultureless person would not be an ape, "but a wholly mindless and consequently unworkable monstrosity" (1973, 68). Here, incidentally, Geertz stresses the co-evolution of brain and culture. "Because tool manufacture puts a premium on manual skill and foresight, its introduction must have acted to shift selection pressures so as to favour the rapid growth of the forebrain as, in all likelihood, did the advances in social organisation, communication and moral regulation which there is reason to believe also occurred during this period of overlap between cultural and biological change" (1973, 67). Geertz appears to give pre-eminence to tool-making, but it may be that communication should claim priority. It has also been suggested that cooperative food gathering, along with information and resource exchange, "may have preceded tool use ... Communication and information exchange may have been more critical than labour and technology in evolving hominids" (Kurland and Beckerman, 1985, 73).*

Other animals may possess certain cultural behaviours, but they are in no sense dependent upon them and this 'culture' in no sense describes, dominates or defines their total behaviour as is the case with humans. Certainly human behaviour is overwhelmingly culturally determined; for the most sophisticated mammal the corresponding proportion of his behaviour would be the consequence of non-cultural factors: either genetic programming or hormonal and nutritional responses to the environment.

Another fundamental difference between human development in culture and that of any animal species is that much of the transmission of human culture from one person to another, especially from one generation to another, entails a conscious and deliberate programme of inculcation. Such non-instinctive and deliberate teaching is primarily a human hallmark. By contrast the diffusion of cultural elements among animals is overwhelmingly by imitation. Animals other than humans seem to have little motivation or capacity to impart learning; innovation spreads because others see and choose to copy.

---

* Hominid refers to the biological family to which humans and their more immediate ancestors such as *Homo erectus* belong. Hominoids are more ancient human-like forms, particularly the Australopithecines.

Concerning culture, the animal world may therefore be divided into three parts:

1) the non-cultural world where animals may learn, but diffusion of an innovation from one individual to another does not seem to occur;

2) the proto-cultural realm where the spread of acquired habits occurs primarily through imitation. Cultural traits are minimal within the total content of behaviours;

3) the cultural world which is the world of humans and others of the genus *Homo* now extinct. Whether the Australopithecines fall into this category is questionable.

Culture: 'reality' and construct

As a concept culture is a construction within the anthropologist's mind developed for the purpose of enhancing understanding of behavioural phenomena. The extent to which a concept clarifies a situation, successfully answers questions and produces new and testable hypotheses are measures of its scientific utility and 'truth'. Presumably a useful concept reflects something of an external reality and its usefulness and 'truth' are directly related to the degree it reflects some 'reality'.

One of the problems in any discipline is the tendency to build constructs and then proceed to lend these a reality they do not in fact have. This is reification or the fallacy of misplaced concreteness. That is, a person observes certain phenomena, abstracts from these observations what he believes to be the important attributes and then employs them to define a concept. The concept as he defines it exists in the investigator's head, not necessarily outside it, but he may proceed to ignore this significant difference, assuming that his construct has reality independent of himself and as he defines it. He concretises the construct or, in other words, misplaces the 'reality' in his own head – the construct – for an external 'reality' outside.

In anthropology the concept of culture is often reified. We often say that culture does this or that or we say that a culture is found in this locality or that particular time. Many treat culture as a market basket which contains these or those objects. Culture is frequently treated or spoken of in the same way one speaks of an elephant or a house. Some anthropologists have even written and spoken as if culture were a gigantic mechanism which operates by itself, independently of humankind. Culture in this view was originally created by humans, but once created it acquires a life of its own, operating according to its own laws. These laws, it is claimed, are studied through a science of culturology, all of which has strange similarities to a kind of animism.

Of course culture actually does nothing. People act. We only infer that they do so because they are motivated by ideas in their heads. We further infer that within a given head these ideas have some degree of integration. It is yet a further and much greater jump on the abstraction ladder to infer that the same ideas are similarly integrated in innumerable heads and so comprise a culture. To say that culture does anything is a shorthand device for saying that individuals are acting thus and so in accord with learned and acquired ideas. This kind of shorthand usage is employed throughout this essay, and most other anthropological writing, but one must always bear in mind that in this text at least it is shorthand.

Culture is a high level of abstraction built from inferences of observed behaviour. It is a term that is similar to numerous others employed in science and in everyday life. Thus, for example, we speak of evolution or of language, both of which are constructs similar to culture. Evolution is neither a concrete entity or something which in fact does anything. It is an abstract concept referring to processes that operate through specific concrete organisms. Such processes as the mutation of genetic material and genetic drift, in consort with the interaction of the organism with its physical environment, produce changes some of which are adaptive for a species. All these several phenomena (and more) are summarised by the construct, evolution (see Diagram 1).

Language as well constitutes an abstract concept of the same order. A language is actually the rules for speaking abstracted by an observer from the particular speech patterns (idiolects) of individuals.

The construction of culture by the anthropologist may operate at different levels. That is, one may undertake an investigation of the way of life of the people of Egypt, executing a series of sample ethnographic studies of villages, towns and cities. We make 'lower' level inferences about the culture of a neighbourhood or a village and then proceed to higher levels in making more general statements pertaining to regions or to the whole country. Possibly a study of a sufficient number of communities coupled with an investigation of Egypt as a 'total' society will allow us to construct an 'Egyptian

Level of abstraction

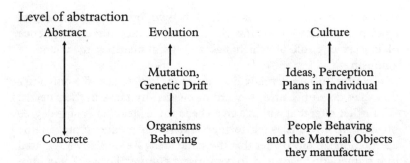

Diagram 1: Evolution and culture compared as high level abstractions

---

culture' and assign rough geographical boundaries to it. And we might even go beyond to even higher and so more abstract levels to tie Egyptian culture up with others and then speak of an Arab culture. All are constructs; all are in a sense inventions or fictions of the anthropologist.

Finally, to say that culture is an anthropological construct does not mean that it is some kind of lie or figment. It is a reality but it is a different kind of reality than, say, that of this chair or even Christianity. What we must be on guard against, whether it is using a concept like culture or evolution or society, is to avoid misplacing the locus of its reality.

Having said this we might note some indications of the culture concept which suggest a reality independent of the anthropological observer. First, many people have a notion that they possess a 'way of life' – a set of beliefs and principles which sets them off from others. Egyptians, for example, recognise an affinity with Syrians, Algerians and others as Arabs. At the same time other groups are recognised as having their own ways of life. This may be a vague feeling not well verbalised, but it indicates a recognition of a cultural reality, independent of the anthropologist's construct. However, one should bear in mind that the notions of the people about their way of life or of others is not necessarily the same as the anthropologist's. Indeed, it can be vastly different.

A second way in which we might attribute an independent reality to culture is in the proposition that a culture is more than the beliefs, plans for action and so forth, bound up inside any given person's head. We have above pointed out how culture is a product of a dialectic process involving the interaction of an individual with the environment. Others, including Geertz and Keesing, have suggested culture entails largely shared meanings which are created and sustained through social interaction. We have a social construction of shared meanings. Each person does not operate through a private conceptualisation of the social world, enacting routines and interpreting meanings on the basis of the private conceptualisation of reality. Culture can entail both a cognitive system within the individual's mind and a system shared within a community. In a similar way a physicist views light in terms of particles and in terms of waves (Keesing, 1981, 98).

Cultural universals

We may ask what, if anything, is universal to all known human groups and to what extent are all these cultural rather than genetically inherited. For various reasons much energy in anthropological circles has been devoted to pointing to the immense diversity of human customs. And, of course, divergence does appear to be the major theme. There are, however, universal attributes shared by all known cultures. At the most general level it has been pointed out that all humans have a developed technology to cope with their environment as they have as well a language, a body of empirical knowledge, a system of beliefs and a social structure with several universal kinds of institutions. But as will be argued again below, these universals are really an inherent part of the definition of what culture is and so are logically obviously universals by definition. The elements which constitute the definition of an entity are universal to the entity in question. There exist nevertheless more specific universals: prohibitions against incest, against making human suffering an end in itself, and against killing or stealing from members of a defined kin group. There are ritualised roles of politeness, hospitality and reciprocity as well as rituals of passage of individuals from one status to another: the funeral is found in some fashion in every human group. Allowing for some leeway in terms of interpretation, several of the ten commandments which God is alleged to have delivered to Moses are universal: there are universal taboos against killing, stealing and lying within at least one's group of close kinsmen and everywhere it is believed that one should 'honour' his father and mother.

Although we may observe that there are certain universals in human culture, they may actually only exist either because they are expressions of the innate nature of the human species and/or because of the innate nature of any kind of social organisation. Thus, for example, no social grouping whether of humans or lions or baboons can persist without there being at the same time some curb on intra-group violence. Numerous ethological studies have demonstrated how various species employ highly standardised genetically programmed techniques for 'social order' within the group. With humans these techniques are cultural in nature. Noam Chomsky argues that a certain deep structure or fundamental logic for language is innate in the human species. If so, there is by extension, assuming language as a part of culture, a 'culture creating facility' inherent in the species as well. There may be a 'deep structure' of culture, a universal logic or pattern upon which all cultures are created and especially in line with the presumed basic socio-psychological characteristics of humanity.

Culture, nation, society and race

There are many terms in common usage which are frequently confused with the anthropological idea of culture. These include nation or country, society and race. Let us consider each of these in turn. Nation and country are political entities, themselves human inventions and so part of culture, but a given nation, a given country, cannot automatically be equated with a culture. One culture may in fact characterise only part of the population of a nation or country; that culture may indeed also characterise the population of two or more countries or parts of two or more countries or it may be roughly contiguous with the boundaries of a single country. In the latter case Icelandic culture is coterminous with the bounds of the Icelandic nation. French culture, on the other hand, is shared by people residing in several different countries, but not all the inhabitants within these countries. Most of the population of the republic of France are culturally French, but there are minorities such as Bretons, Germans, Basques and Corsicans dwelling there as well. A large minority of the population of Switzerland is French, as is also that of Canada, although they would be seen as very definitely representing sub-cultural variants of French culture. In a third case, Arab culture covers most of North Africa as well as the Arabian Peninsula: a common Arab culture again with several regional variants prevails in more than twenty separate nations. Culture does not equal nation or country, but there is strong pressure for those in one nation or country to become homogenised into a single culture which is invariably that of the politically and economically dominant population within it.

Culture is also confused with society. Culture, as we have noted, is a complex of learned ideas characterising a population; society is a group of individual organisms who live in a condition of rather stable interaction and interdependence with one another and are residents of some specific place in space and time. They also interact more with others of their society than with those outside it. Individual humans who constitute a society ordinarily will have a common culture or variants of a common culture, but this need not be the case. Especially division of the modern world into a number of different nations or nation-states produces a situation which compels those in one nation to interact more, and become more interdependent with others in that nation than with those outside. Consequently, society increasingly becomes coterminous with a nation or country, although the implication of the term nation is different from that of society. It has already been observed that nation suggests the political order of things; society suggests the broader more inclusive ordering of all social relations: political, family, economic and so forth. And such an ordering of social relations would usually be defined by a specific culture.

In addition there have been, and remain, numerous operative societies which do not constitute nations or states. One may readily think of the Nuer in the southern Sudan. There is a Nuer culture and a Nuer society but there never was a Nuer nation. That is, Nuer are characterised by shared culture and enduring and stable social interaction and interdependence which constitutes a society, but Nuer have never had a centralised political integration, a concept of central government and territorial national sovereignty which would allow us to say there was any Nuer nation.

Finally, we consider culture and race, two terms which are even further apart than either of the foregoing. Unfortunately they are all too commonly confused. Every day we encounter people who make reference to an English, French, German, even Jewish race. This is diametrically counter to any acceptable anthropological usage. For a race is a biological term referring to a sub-species. A race is a group of individuals within a species which possesses certain distinguishing characteristics all of which are inherited through the genetic material. The population may be said to breed true to these characteristics which distinguish them and which are stable within the population.

As shall be further explored on pages 42-46 in the discussion of the theory of racial determinism, race has very little if anything at all to do with culture and should then be totally divorced from it. In other words, the difference between a German and an Englishman has nothing whatever to do with race, but it has a lot to do with culture. German and English refer either to cultural or national affiliation. Being German, being Jewish or Nuer or Chinese is acquired by learning; it is a cultural phenomenon. However, for many people these issues are, depending on one's point of view, either hopelessly confused or stirling clear when it comes to distinguishing Englishmen from an East Indian or a Sub-Saharan African. Here we find apparent differences both in custom or habits of behaving and in physical appearance or phenotype. But any of these biological features is completely independent of the cultural ones as is clearly evidenced for example by the *very* English 'black' man whose ancestry is from Africa or the West Indies or the likewise very English 'brown' man whose ancestry is from India. Or conversely, we have evidence of the pink-skinned light-haired folks in Europe who, despite physical similarities, have quite different cultures.

Bibliography

Ernst Cassirer, *An Essay on Man* (Doubleday Anchor, New York, 1954).

Noam Chomsky, *Language and Mind* (Harcourt Brace Jovanovich, New York, 1972).

Noam Chomsky, *Reflections on Language* (Pantheon, New York, 1975).

Clifford Geertz, *The Interpretation of Cultures* (Basic Books, New York, 1973).

Ward H. Goodenough, *Culture, Language and Society* (Benjamin Cummings, Menlo Park, California, 1981).

Roger Keesing, *Cultural Anthropology: A Contemporary View* (second edition, Holt, Rinehart & Winston, New York, 1981).

Clyde Kluckhohn and W.H. Kelly, 'The Concept of Culture' in *The Science of Man in the World of Crisis* edited by Ralph Linton (Columbia University Press, New York, 1945).

Ralph Linton, *The Study of Man* (Appleton-Century-Crofts, New York, 1936).

Wilhelm Ostwald, 'The Modern Theory of Energetics' in *The Monist* (1907).

2.
The Dynamics of Culture

Innovation

Culture in general is primarily a conservative force. Or, more correctly, the great majority of those who share a common culture have some interest in perpetuating it unchanged. This is particularly so of those who have become successful within the cultural framework; others as well are likely to be equally conservative. They have grown up with certain traditions and have become so accustomed to them that they are like a second nature. The world of the known and the familiar has its pain and misfortune, but it is a known and therefore somewhat predictable world with at least some benign characteristics. Utopia, no matter how pleasant it may sound, still is an unknown gamble. Humans as creatures of habit are more often conservatives who will tolerate a considerable amount of abuse before actually attempting to alter existing conditions and explore new techniques. In addition, the very notion of abuse itself is a largely culturally relative one. Whereas some may perceive a particular situation as abusive, others will not.

It takes a lot to get people to change, but people do change; cultures change. If one of the universal characteristics of culture is conservatism and resistance to change another is its antinomy: the continual tendency to change.

Change does not occur uniformly across all aspects or within all institutions of a given culture, nor do all the cultures change at the same rate or in the same respects. Amongst cultures of the European tradition, including North America, there has developed a positive attitude towards the most rapid change within the technological realm. Part of the values of North American and European cultures favour rapid technological change towards allegedly ever more efficient 'up to date' forms. A 'horse and buggy' style is now totally unacceptable. At the same time North Americans and Europeans do not look as favourably upon change in other realms of culture. Among North Americans, for example, suggestions of some rapid change in economic institutions, or in the political system or family arrangements are met with a stony glare. And while they may not exhibit much close attachment to it, most North Americans and Europeans still have strong emotional ties to a religion which is two thousand years old. The same people who insist on a technology of the twenty-first century also insist upon a religion of the first century, a political and economic system of the eighteenth, a family system of the tenth century and an attitude towards the settlement of disputes which is 50,000 years old.

By way of contrast the aboriginal populations of Australia have been very conservative in their technology and comparatively innovative in their social organisation and religious system. For centuries they changed their technological system most imperceptibly and primarily by stylistic modifications on a very limited range of tools, particularly projectiles. By contrast these people have invented a variety of different kinship-based forms of social organisation, a rich and elaborate ritual system and an equally complex mythology.

Not only does the process of change vary from one group to another in terms of what is acceptable for change, but change occurs as well by fits and starts. Egypt is an appropriate example here. For most of the first three thousand years of its existence as a state and civilisation, one of the distinguishing features of its culture was stability and the persistence of tradition. Change occurred so very slowly that one might be misled into believing this was an absolutely static period. About the beginning of the Christian era, however, and down to about the twelfth century there followed an era which experienced a considerable number of ideological and organisational alterations. It was a period of great flux related, among other things, to the impact of Greek, Christian, Gnostic and finally Muslim thought. Then more static and unchanging times followed and persisted to the beginning of the nineteenth century at which time Egypt entered and continues to remain in another period of very rapid cultural change.

Anthropologists have generally seen the process of change as primarily involving two basic mechanisms: innovation and diffusion. Innovation, which, following Homer Barnett, includes both invention and discovery alike, is the combination of two or more cultural items so as to form some new pattern or form – some new combination of elements (1953, 7). The automobile was an invention which basically combined the idea of an internal combustion engine with a four-wheeled wagon so that the wheels would be driven by the energy from the machine.

Discoveries, too, are similar combinations, although in common usage a discovery is ordinarily different from an invention. Discovery is believed to be the finding of some pattern which already exists in nature but had heretofore not been noticed or appreciated. Thus it has been said that humans discovered fire, rather than invented it, because fire and its manufacture already existed in nature and it was up to humans eventually to perceive its significance and how it is manufactured. Matches would, however, be an invention because they are a novel combination of elements to produce fire and they are so combined by the human inventor. We also say that Columbus discovered America. This is a slightly different usage, since it really means that Europeans, or perhaps non-Scandinavian Europeans, first encountered the existence of this continent. The Amerindians had been aware of it for 30,000 or more years.

Discoveries can become inventions. That is, presumably Ptolemy discovered that the earth was the centre of the universe, but later Copernicus and Galileo discovered a totally different relationship of earth to the universe and relegated the Ptolemaic system to being an invention.

Notions of invention and discovery can both be included under the single term innovation since both entail the same essential elements of combining old and existent ideas into new forms. In the case of discovery the act of innovation is a matter of first noticing the significance of some already existent combinations of items in nature.

It is a common misconception to identify inventions or innovations with tools alone. The prototype of our notion of the 'inventor' is Thomas Alva Edison, a man who made the first electric light and phonograph machine. In fact, Jesus Christ or Buddha, Plato or Karl Marx or the originator of Esperanto or Pig Latin, the unknown person who first practised polyandry or infanticide – all of these are inventors or innovators. Innovation relates to modifications in the total realm of culture, not technology alone. After all, all culture, all languages, dialects and idiolects, the countless religions and philosophical systems, kinship arrangements, political systems and economic arrangements have been invented by some human somewhere. And as we have had occasion to mention several times before in this essay, each of us is in his own way a modest innovator. Each of us may be inculcated with a culture, but we modify it and so create something different and new. I may speak the English language and even a dialect of that language, but I also speak an idiolect of that language that is peculiar to me: I have developed habitual patterns of grammatical constructions, a particular vocabulary and manner of pronunciation which in their totality is something unique to me, created by me.

Innovations are not for the most part products of conscious effort, nor are innovations so often products of necessity. Innovation as conscious effort seems more a recent development as large corporations appropriate increasingly greater sums for research and have helped turn invention into a specialised profession. Most of the inventions of the past have been by-products of accident or play and even many modern innovations are derived from these sources, e.g. vulcanisation was an accident; rocketry developed out of play.

It is a common folk belief that necessity is the mother of invention, when the reverse of this is just as true. For example, it might be argued that humans invented roofs over buildings because they felt the need to cover themselves from the elements, but the question arises, when would they have felt this need. Humans went for a long time without them and without therefore feeling the need. The main problem with the argument for invention out of necessity is that it is ex-post facto: once we have the advantage of the invention and therefore appreciate its 'necessity' we can readily speculate that it was invented out of necessity when in fact the felt necessity does not arise until after the fact, that is after the invention is in use.

We might reverse the old folk notion and just as readily say that invention is the mother of necessity. That is to suggest not only that we can always find a rationale for an invention once it has been made, but that the invention itself provokes a host of new needs themselves. Once roofs are invented there are inventions to insulate them, to develop a variety of shingling devices, to install windows or other openings in them, to give them different styles of construction, and so on.

Innovation is the basic mechanism of cultural change: one has to have a novel idea before change can occur. But innovation is dependent on diffusion. Innovation which is to have any cultural impact and is to be incorporated into the cultural milieu must be accepted at least by some people and in some fashion. As has been said, everyone is an innovator in some modest way; most remain innovators in this very modest fashion because what we invent is never accepted by anyone else or only by a few people. An innovation which remains the private and peculiar practice or view of its inventor is idiosyncratic and therefore has little significance in cultural analysis. The spread or diffusion of the idea is therefore of crucial importance. Diffusion occurs within a specified cultural group and then also items are spread from one culture to another.

Acculturation

The world of the last 300-400 years has experienced a considerable amount of rapid and widespread diffusion, chiefly of ideas spread by western Europeans. This rapid and intense diffusion has been largely from powerful, expansionist and predatory peoples to militarily weaker ones, a major consequence of which is revolutionary or fundamental change in the latter cultures. Such a rapid diffusion process which is primarily characterised by the spread of ideas from the more powerful to the less powerful peoples is called acculturation. Although acculturation has an emphatic unidirectional character, one should not lose sight of the fact that traits also pass during this process from the least powerful to the powerful. Many American Indians have become so acculturated to an Anglo-American style culture that they have few of their Indian traditions remaining. Nevertheless, a listing here of all the myriad of traits of Indian origin which have been incorporated into the Anglo-American culture would become tedious indeed.

Although the acculturation process produces radical changes in cultures it sometimes ends in assimilation where one of the cultures in the contact situation (invariably the least powerful one) totally disappears as people abandon their traditions and adopt those of the dominant culture. Several American Indian groups in the eastern United States have been thus assimilated. But in the Mongol conquests of China, Chinese culture eventually prevailed as the invaders, for all intents and purposes, became Chinese. In some other situations two peoples representing different cultural traditions encounter one another and the results, despite the military conquest of one by the other, are essentially a disappearance of both cultures as a perceptibly new one is created within this milieu. Perhaps the Norman Conquest of Anglo-Saxon England and the resultant English culture is a case in point.

Functionalism

Many anthropologists spending their lives investigating cultures which were undergoing the acculturation process came to imply that this, or at least some diffusion of elements from outside the culture, was the way in which cultures always changed. These anthropologists assumed a functionalist view of culture which held that every culture is an integrated whole the parts of which are all harmoniously related so as to produce a condition of balance or equilibrium. What caused disharmony and disruptions in this otherwise balanced system was a product of external forces – indeed it could only be from outside since if the 'normal' system was a balanced one there was nothing within which could account for something which would provoke imbalance and thus change. This model one can see might readily appeal to an anthropologist who is making a study of some 'primitive' or archaic community which has no written history of its past and has now been faced with recent European intrusions. In this kind of situation one might well be misled into believing that prior to European contact the world of such people was an integrated and harmonious one which never changed and what causes the disruption is the massive assault from outside.

Such functionalist thinking, however, has numerous shortcomings. No one will disagree with the functionalists in holding that integration is a feature of culture. That is, there is some kind of harmonious inter-relationship between most cultural elements. But it is apparent that any culture can survive a considerable amount of disintegration and that there is no reason to assume that prior to European invasions these numerous cultures were harmonious wholes. Functionalism implies that an isolated group unaffected by the outside world would never change. Or in other words, it assumes that there is nothing in the internal dynamics of a social system or structure which can provoke change. This view is in need of radical modification.

Cultures change from external influences (e.g. acculturation) and they change from internal forces as well. Cultures do not, as the functionalist model implies, operate as machines. Any culture is only more or less integrated; it has functionally related parts and it has other elements which may be dysfunctional or in conflict with the main thrust of the system as well as elements which apparently have no discernible function.

Conflict theory
It cannot be forgotten that a culture is only manifest through the individual behaviour of its participants and in no culture are those participants clones. In every system there is variation in terms of behaviour and interpretation of behaviour. And this situation provides then the opportunity for conflict. Conflict is likewise inherent within a system of authority and within any social arrangement there seems to be some rivalry for power and influence which has the potential for generating conflict. Human societies universally involve individuals

with differential access to power and influence. Out of such a situation arises friction and resentment, producing conflict. And this in turn may eventually provoke pressure for change. Thus, a socio-cultural system may clearly change as a result of internal dynamics and need not depend purely on external stimuli for this to occur. It may be seen in functional and structural terms, but it is also a potential source of conflict and thus a generator of change.

Some kind of conflict theory is necessary to account fully for cultural change. A common one today, largely made so through Marxism, is a dialectic theory. Here it is argued that an existing set of conditions (a thesis) provokes its own opposing position (an antithesis) and the resulting conflict between the two will be resolved in some kind of synthesis – a new situation.

This approach in general seems a fruitful one. Yet it has distinct limitations. First, there is no reason to believe that in every cultural system conflicting positions *must* be resolved. Cultures persist for long periods while tolerating unresolved conflicts. In fact it has been said that a culture may persist by riding, so to speak, on its internal conflicts. It achieves a kind of dynamic equilibrium through the balanced opposition of the conflicting forces. Probably one of the first to recognise this phenomenon was Pierre Proudhon (see DeLubac, 1948, 140 ff).

Secondly, granting the eventual resolution of a conflict there may not necessarily be a synthesis. This term suggests that the new order is not only derived from the conflicting forces alone, but that there are approximately equal parts of each involved in its creation. However, it might be that a conflict is resolved by an innovation which has a variety of sources. Or perhaps the 'antithesis' will merely replace the thesis.

Thirdly, the dialectic triad of thesis, antithesis and synthesis is so ambiguous that it allows for all kinds of equally plausible explanations. The famous Marxian dialectic proffered the thesis of capitalism which generated its antithesis, the proletariat, and the ensuing conflict of these is presumably resolved in the synthesis, socialism and finally communism. (It is, incidentally, also interesting to note that Marxism is only partially a conflict theory and only partially applies the dialectic explanation, since once communism is attained conflict and dialectic apparently occur no longer; society becomes a harmonious integrated whole after the model of the discredited functionalists.)

But the more fundamental problem with this 'explanation' is with what constitutes the 'antithesis' and 'thesis'. We may readily grant that capitalism of some kind has been an existent state of affairs and that it has certainly generated considerable hostility in many quarters. There is a conflict between 'capitalists' and 'proletarians' (wage workers). We might then say, while remaining within the context of the dialectic, that this struggle between these classes produces a conflicting ideology, an antithesis which is socialism, and that in turn the opposition between the thesis (capitalism) and the antithesis (socialism) is a synthesis (fascism) in which fascism among other things combines the capitalist idea of private ownership of property with the socialist idea of government control.*

This 'explanation' seems to have some accord with the historical conditions. While we would not call the large modern states, from the United States to the Soviet Union, fascist, they do exhibit a trend towards more powerful and enormous centralised bureaucracies whether in government or in the corporation, more state control and more interlocking of state and corporate enterprise, and reduced liberty.

Not all cultural change can be explained by the dialectic process or by conflict theory in general. But these are nevertheless essentials. A dialectic analysis applied with care and precision can shed light on issues of cultural dynamics.

Cultural change through abandonment and loss

Interesting facets of innovation and diffusion are changes by abandonment or loss or alteration in meaning and function. The introduction of some new innovation often has the effect of causing existing practices to be given up or at least of causing modification in their use and meaning. The adoption of the electric light clearly altered the meaning and function of candles, which a hundred years ago served as mundane sources of light, but now are employed for festive, ritual or emergency occasions. Sixty years ago horses were the main source of traction on American farms. With the development of the tractor and truck, horses declined so rapidly that some predicted their extinction. However, a major revival in horse numbers commenced about twenty years ago so that today they have increased threefold, but now are primarily for pleasure and recreation purposes. At the same time, the once important

---

* The central thesis of fascism is the absolute supremacy of the state over all institutions and organisations and the subordination of the individual to it.

crafts of horse collar and harness maker and buggy and wagon manufacturer have come to the brink of extinction (Barclay, 1980). Canoes, sleds, toboggans, tents are all only a few of the numerous cultural elements which were once practical tools, but today are preserved almost entirely in the realms of recreation.

A great number of practices have been abandoned by people without their necessarily being replaced by something else. In many societies hanging has been abolished but it has not been replaced by another form of capital punishment. Few societies today practice public floggings or other public punishments. Head hunting and scalping are in rapid decline. In Western medicine bleeding, the use of leeches and other archaic practices have been abandoned. Such changes have often been induced by the acceptance of new innovations which have made these ideas redundant or in overt conflict with the new innovation.

Abandonment and loss or change in meaning and function need not necessarily occur solely because some innovation has been adopted which displaces another. Abandonment and loss may in part be attributable to factors internal to the nature of the existing social system. Zoroastrianism is the ancient Iranian religion still adhered to by a few thousand followers mainly in Iran and India. Among other things the religion is characterised by an hereditary priesthood and an extremely complex set of rituals which can only be performed by the priests. As Zoroastrianism has declined in recent decades there has not only occurred a decline in the priesthood but also in the transmission of rituals from the older generation of priests to the younger, so that rituals are consequently being lost or abandoned. There are many Zoroastrian communities where certain ceremonies are no longer performed because there are no qualified personnel who know how to perform them. The extinction of the class of priests would literally be the extinction of Zoroastrianism (*cf.* Boyce).

Kroeber reports several examples of the loss of useful arts. On Torres Island in Melanesia canoes disappeared from the island tradition because the families specialised in their manufacture died out. Eskimos in northern Greenland lacked kayaks because of the absence of driftwood in their region. And once they were able to acquire wood, there was no longer anyone among them who knew how to make these boats (Kroeber, 1948, 375).

Theories of cultural dynamics

One of the influences of modern science upon the several social studies has been to emphasise explanatory theories which try to reduce explanations to the simplest common denominator. Another influence has been to stress 'materialistic' causes. Consequently most of the theories of cultural dynamics which have been in vogue from time to time have sought to reduce the explanation of cultural data to the influences of some single major material entity or factor. In this section I propose to deal briefly with these theories and at the same time to argue that cultural phenomena should be explained in terms of cultural phenomena and as parts of an interrelated system which should take into account the causal significance of the several components and not merely one or two.

The several single factor-materialist theories of cultural dynamics are basically of two different kinds. There are those which look to extra cultural factors and seek to reduce the cultural to the non-cultural. These include demographic, environmental – that is, geographical – and racial theories. Another set of explanatory theories does not seek to reduce or explain away culture in terms of some simpler level of phenomena. Rather these seek to explain all culture in terms of its so-called infrastructure – some basic aspect or institution of the culture. The super-structure then is a by-product of that infrastructure – an epiphenomenal feature built on to the basic causal 'reality'. Such theories have invariably taken either the economic institution or the technology, or both together, as the ultimate frame of reference or infrastructure.

These theories share in common the attempt to explain cultural phenomena in terms of one, or at best a select few, material factors and to relegate other factors to a superficial position as their by-products. As such they are reductionist and reductionist in an overly simplistic fashion. The aims of science to reduce phenomena to as simple and as few explanatory variables as is possible is clearly commendable, yet it is quite apparent as well that there are limits to this reductionist process. Ideally it might be desirable if we could account for all phenomena by a few laws of physics. This would mean that such laws should then generate and account for the nature of everything. If human behaviour can be reduced to physical laws this means that physical laws should be able to explain fully and hence predict human behaviour.

We know this cannot be done; we know as well that even biological generalisations are unable to account fully for human behaviour. The creation of a multitude of sciences and academic disciplines speaks to the limitations of reducing data to some common simplest explainable terms. Thus, biology and its several branches appear and legitimate themselves because living matter – life itself as a reorganisation of materials at a new and discrete level of phenomena – is not explainable by laws of physics alone. Precisely because it is a new organisation of materials above and beyond the laws of physics, new techniques of analysis, causal processes and the like must be brought to bear.

Living material as an emergent requires a special science with its own explanatory procedures and generalisations. In the same manner human behaviour becomes divisible into several separate fields because even though humans are living organisms, biology, like physics and chemistry, lacks the techniques, concepts and procedures to explain that behaviour. Human behaviour and culture itself are emergents as well. Perhaps it should be made clear that psychology also lacks the ability to explain human culture and that is why it is that there are cultural sciences, including anthropology.

Aside from reductionism, these theories share in common a considerable dependence upon *ex post facto* analysis. The conditions already have existed, an action may have long since been completed, and the investigator is left to look back after the fact and surmise how the present arose out of the past. One is always left with trying to decide which of the many possibilities is the most plausible explanation, but one cannot know or 'prove' the true one.

Except for racial theory, which has nothing to commend it, these theories do share some degree of truth. That is, cultural dynamics cannot be fully understood unless one does consider the role of population size and growth. Geographical factors of climate, soil type and terrain, flora and fauna additionally cannot be ignored. The same may be said about economic and technological explanations and combinations of the demographic-geographic-economic-technological – the so-called cultural materialist view. The latter attempts to overcome the single factor emphasis of similar theories, but like them it is dedicated to a materialistic position which categorically rejects the thesis that ideas are causal and can be anything other than by-products of 'material' demands. Regardless of the truth each may contain, they are still to be faulted as over-simplified and as ignoring too much else to be acceptable.

Racial theory

The view that cultural variation and cultural achievement and success is directly related to and a consequence of biological race continues to persist among laymen as a part of their folk ideology. Modern anthropology, on the other hand, has totally rejected this theory. First, racial theory ought to be contingent upon the development of a most precise concept of race as it applies to *Homo sapiens*. What the significant criteria of a human race might be, what and how many human races there are, if any, have been issues which have confronted physical anthropology since its inception. Without going into the complex history of the matter here it may be pointed out that there is simply no consensus among specialists as to whether, to begin with, humanity is divisible into races. Further, amongst those who would accept racial differentiation in our species as a fact, there is no agreement about what these races are. Those who hold to a racial division of humankind concede that at best racial characteristics define populations, but individuals, as individuals, cannot all be pegged in one race or the other. Racial characteristics at best are statistical tendencies and in no sense absolutes.

Human populations have been mixing for thousands of years so that one population blends into another and there are no distinct boundaries which permit the establishment of discrete races. There are of course geographical centres throughout the globe for each of a couple of dozen traits that have been employed to characterise racial groups. In each centre there is the highest concentration of persons having a given physical feature, but as one moves from the centre the proportion declines as a contrasting feature or features increase in prevalence.

Finally, each of the presumed racial features are of quite minor importance, particularly in their contemporary role in human survival or as regards intelligence or creative potential. The human population has drawn practically all of its characteristics, and certainly any that are important, from the same common pool of genetic material. Race can at best be of only the most peripheral importance in understanding our species. Since the concept actually creates more difficulties than it solves, both in terms of biological understanding and in terms of human social relationships, an increasing number of anthropologists have come to the conclusion that the racial concept is best abandoned.

No solid conception of race among *Homo sapiens* has ever been presented and the advocates of a racial determinism have been among the worst in their loose usage of the term. Indeed, it is clear that they could have no theory at all if their race concept was in any sense precise.

Granting, for the sake of argument, that races are discernible and meaningful categories among *Homo sapiens*, any racial theory suffers from the further problem of associating cultural development with one race or another. It is not a mystery that the great colonisers and imperialists of the modern world originating in Europe evolved racial theories advocating the supremacy of a 'white' race. Yet the derivation of such racist conclusions from the broad sweep of history and prehistory can only be made by the application to the record of the most outrageous bias.

Perhaps some nineteenth century European scholar might be forgiven for perceiving the world and history from a Mediterranean perspective such that he was unfamiliar with other parts of the earth, and so drew out evidence which might lend itself to a doctrine of racial determinism and of 'white' supremacy. Certainly no global view of human cultural achievement could possibly lead to such conclusions. In brief, a global view would clearly show that each human 'racial' group has produced a variety of different kinds of cultural expression. And, at the same time, it would demonstrate that members of different racial stocks have contributed to the development of the same culture. Thus, members of the so-called 'black' race have produced an immense variety of different kinds of culture over the course of time. At the same time they have participated with other races, especially 'whites', in producing single cultures, as for example in the United States and Brazil. These two points are of crucial significance because if, as traditional racial determinists argue, race is the primary or sole determinant of cultural achievement, then it follows that all the people of the same race should produce the same invariant culture. Therefore, since Spaniards and Albanians are both Mediterranean type 'whites' they both should have the same culture, or since Chinese and Kazaks are of the 'mongoloid' or 'yellow' race they too should have the same culture. Or conversely, persons from different racial stocks could not produce the same culture.

In order for a racial explanation of culture to make sense one would have to say that those who share a specific culture constitute a discrete race. This would be a totally indefensible and downright ridiculous position. To argue along such lines would mean that each culture would have to remain a homogeneous and undifferentiated whole since there also would be no room in the racial theory for providing for the appearance of cultural variation unless there was at the same time racial variation. Thus, any sub-cultural variation would be impossible. Indeed, racial determinism is a logical absurdity since each person is in some respect culturally unique, in which case since race is presumed to cause culture every individual would be a separate race.

Clearly of all the single factor determinist theories, racial theory receives the lowest grade as an explanatory device. In no way can one explain the product (culture) from the alleged cause (race). It is unfortunate that racism continues today not only among laymen but also as a thinly disguised academic theory particularly attempting to relate race to intelligence – and of course that is essentially what the earlier racialists were interested in. They wished to demonstrate that one race (white) was the most intelligent by attempting to show the meagreness of cultural achievement amongst others.

In recent attempts to tie race to intelligence much of the investigation hinges upon a racial distinction between 'whites' and 'blacks' in the United States. This alone is a most dubious distinction since both populations have been interbreeding ever since they settled in this hemisphere, so as to confound completely any attempt to measure the causal role of such a concept as race. Then, in addition, there is the ambiguous question of what is intelligence and, even more, the means by which it should be measured. In sum the case for a causal relationship between something called race and intelligence as with the relationship to culture is highly suspect. And in both cases this is not only related to the concepts and other methodological techniques of inquiry which are applied, but also to the ideological implications. Indeed, if we had to concern ourselves with the scientific worth of racist theories alone they could readily be ignored as being crackpot, but it is because such theories pose a real political force for scapegoating and for attempts at various kinds of domination, and even downright genocide, that they must be continually addressed, taken seriously and exposed.

We often hear of individuals who are accused of being 'racists' not only because they make derogatory remarks about 'blacks' or 'Orientals', but about Jews or Ukrainians or Hispanics as well. In this case racist and racism have been expanded to include not only references to biological race, but also to ethnic and ethnic/religious affiliation. This, as we have already pointed out, is an example of a confusion of race with culture. The perpetuation of such a confusion has its origins in the teachings of earlier racial theories and in folk anthropology.

Probably the most notorious in this regard were the Nazi views on race. Nazism promoted the notion that the Jews were a race and an inferior one at that. It appropriated the name of an essentially linguistic grouping, Aryan, and made it a race. It may be largely in response to such confusion that opponents of Nazism and other racist theories commenced employing the words racist and racism in the much looser and general sense.

There is another reason why racism has become expanded to refer not only to presumed biological races but to ethnic groups as well. The individual racist draws various conclusions and makes prejudiced statements about both kinds of groups because of certain myths and stereotypes that are built up about them. Invariably the racist draws these conclusions because he wishes to reinforce his own belief in his group's superiority and because 'out-groups', especially those which are visible through distinctive physical features or dress patterns, are effective targets for venting hostilities and being 'scapegoats'.

Now it may be that the expanded usage of racism and racist can be justified on the grounds that derogatory statements are still derogatory whether applied to a 'race' or an ethnic community. Yet, to repeat, it perpetuates a confounding of biology and culture ... of what is inherited and what is acquired. And this contains some potentially difficult implications. On the one hand, derogatory remarks about groups defined by certain physical characteristics – 'races' – refer to the inherited characteristics over which the individual has no control and for which there is no evidence that they make any difference in the ability or behaviour of individuals anyway. On the other hand, similar remarks and assessments concerning groups defined by cultural characteristics – ethnic or ethnic/religious groups – have their ultimate referent in acquired or learned traits. Here the individual does have some control over how he behaves and what he believes. Further there is an immense body of evidence to demonstrate that these learned attributes and beliefs have a great deal to do with a person's ability and behaviour.

In any free society it is taken for granted that the merits of different beliefs and behaviours are subject for open debate. So we come down to the fine line of what is legitimate debate concerning the merits of this or that belief and what is 'racist' insult. Some, taking what is a cultural relativist position, say rather unthinkingly that no one may criticise the beliefs and practises of anyone else because that is racist. In Canadian and American society it is common to hear that one should not criticise another's religion. This incidentally suggests another element in the confusion of race and culture. Race, of course, is biologically inherited, while religion, since most people invariably follow the religion of their parents and their parents before them, therefore gives the appearance of being inherited as well. Thus perhaps the notion here is that one should not criticise that which is 'inherited'.

Be that as it may, we cannot abdicate the free debate about varying beliefs and behaviours because some may confuse this with 'racism', nor can we accept racism disguised as a free debate about beliefs. It is not always easy to distinguish a legitimate from a racist argument. Those who have criticised Zionism have been accused of being racist anti-Semites. But Zionism is a social-political philosophy – like socialism or anarchism – and, like them, must be subject to critical analysis and this must be divorced from an argument against Zionism for racist reasons.

In general a racist argument can be quite subtle, but ordinarily it entails blatant exaggeration and distortion if not falsehood; it misplaces causal relations; it offers dogmatic, unsubstantiated statements and gross generalisations. A telling characteristic of any racist is that the racist condemns out of hand a whole group because of some alleged characteristics he does not particularly like. What is involved is no principle but a matter of taste and a matter of condemnation of that which to him is different, and so a good object for the venting of hostility. In his condemnation the racist scoffs at and denigrates people; he is unconcerned with the debate of ideas.

Sociobiology

Since the early 1970s another theory of biological-genetic causation has become popular in certain academic circles. This orientation known as sociobilogy tends to a biological reductionism especially to the extent that its less cautious protagonists see genetic programming as an adequate explanation of human behaviour.

We have noted that all humans share certain very general kinds of behaviour in common. There are universals, in other words. We note that all humans as 'social'; they can be aggressive as well as 'altruistic'. Sociobiologists contend that important features of human behaviour are genetically programmed. They argue, for example, that there is a gene for altruism and it has survival value since by altruistic acts one helps his kinsmen so they they multiply and in so doing increase the bearers of genes similar to one's own.

That certain important human behaviours are both universal and appear to have survival value would seem to suggest that they may have some broad genetic basis. At the same time whether or not there are one or more genes for altruism or other similar behavioural attributes and what type of gene they might be remains purely conjectural since no one has as yet isolated them. Secondly, even if there were such genes, we still could not say that they in any way explain how it is that we have such a myriad of varying expressions of, for instance, altruism in the human species. We cannot, in other words, reduce the observable human behaviour to a biological explanation. Genetics may be the foundation stone, but it is the historically derived and learned ideas – culture – which creates the complex edifice which thereby allows us to understand the variety of human behaviour around the globe. We require the concept of culture to explain how it is that altruism can be expressed in such a multitude of forms.

Finally, sociobiologists place great emphasis on their 'explanation' that traits persist because they have survival value for the species or for certain gene combinations. But what really does such an explanation tell us? I believe that sociobiology betrays the same problems as the older and largely discredited functionalism. That is, the 'explanation' is not only reductionist, but also an *ex post facto* or 'after the fact' argument. And it is above all a circular argument: a trait survives because it persists. Among other things, we are offered no account as to why in a given case any one of several alternatives might not be just as viable since such an account would not be a biological-genetic one, but a cultural historical one. At the same time it adds little to our understanding to observe that humans have, for example, aggressive tendencies. What is far more important is the way these tendencies are expressed and that demands a cultural explanation.*

Geographical determinism

Much of what we may call folk anthropology – that is, theorising by the layman on human behaviour – often relies unfortunately on some kind of racial theory or on geographical determinism or both.

---

* Two major statements of the sociobiological position are *Sociobiology: The New Synthesis* (Harvard University Press, Cambridge, Massachusetts, 1975) and *On Human Nature* (Harvard University Press, Cambridge, Massachusetts, 1978) both by Edward O. Wilson.

Geographical determinism is the view that culture is explainable as a response to physical environment; culture is an adaptive device of humans to achieve this end or, in other words, culture is a by-product of the physical environment. This kind of approach argues, for example, that Inuit living in Arctic conditions therefore would live in snow houses, would wear fur clothing and would also be seal and walrus hunters. Such an argument suffers from problems similar to some of those associated with racist theory. Both, of course, are based upon *ex post facto* analysis: we have already the alleged results before us and now must try to surmise the possible causes. Consequently we may arrive at any number of plausible explanations, none of which, by the way, are provable. Further, another problem applying to racism also applies to geographical determinism, viz., if the geographical conditions are the determinants of culture, then the same invariant forms of culture should be found in the same geographical conditions. That is, everyone who lives in the Arctic should live in a snow house, should wear fur clothing and hunt seals and walruses. But this is not so. Not even all Inuit used the igloo and clearly people of European extraction live in Arctic areas in totally different kinds of houses, wearing clothes of wool and synthetic materials and eating quite different kinds of food.

Another brief example is the desert area of the Arizona and New Mexico region. This same geographical area traditionally supported American Indian cultures of quite diverse forms: the agricultural village-dwelling Pueblo people and hunting-gathering nomadic Apachean people.

The significance of geographical factors is a constraining one. Humans are essentially tropical animals. As such if they are to reside in an Arctic environment they must have some form of shelter, some form of warm clothing and fire; if they are not to be dependent upon outside supplies they would find it extremely difficult to survive without reliance upon hunting wild game on land and sea. These are specific limits which are set, but within them there is opportunity for choice, for innovation and variation, and these are up to the ingenuity of the human population. Of course in a land such as the Arctic the choices are the most limited and restrictive of anywhere in the world and this area is most conducive to geographical environmentalist explanations.

Much cultural variation still occurs, however, that is not at all explainable in these terms, especially when one considers language, religion, kinship system and political organisation. We note that they can reflect the geographical environment, but not necessarily. What of the environment determines the grammar of Inuit language or the phonemic system? Russian, Chinese, English or, indeed, Hausa are just as 'efficient' languages in the Arctic as Inuit. Living in the northern conditions might require, particularly for Hausa, the addition of a few words and lead to the abandonment of others, but these are minor or peripheral alterations.

People of varying religions are found in all kinds of geographical zones. There is none in which Christianity, which originated in a sub-tropical semi-arid zone, cannot be found. Islam, originating in a similar geography, is almost as equally widespread. Communism is a political-economic system spread today from Tropics to Arctic. Political systems and kinship systems alike ignore geography. What anthropologists refer to as an Eskimo type kinship system is not only found in some parts of the Arctic (among most Eskimos) but is also a general feature of European peoples whether they reside in Europe, America, Australia or Africa. In short there are a vast number of areas within cultures whose distribution cannot be explained in any way by geographical environment.

In addition, geographical determinists have too frequently overlooked the ways in which humankind alters and determines the geography. The last two decades have impressed upon all of us the extent to which humans have polluted the lands and waters of the globe, forced many species into extinction, enhanced the extent of desert on the earth and even threatened to destroy the whole earth in nuclear holocaust.

In sum, geographical factors impose certain boundaries on cultural development. This is only a small part of the total story which must also include the active role of human ingenuity.

Demographic determinism

Demographic determinism seeks to explain cultural dynamics in terms of population size, concentrations, pressures and changes. Plant and animal domestication are sometimes accounted for as a response to increasing population in a restricted area. The origin of the state can also be similarly accounted for. Population pressures do call for cultural response but, as in the case of environmental determination, it is not the population pressure which specifies the precise nature of the cultural response. Population, like environment, is a limiting factor within which humans experiment and innovate.

Furthermore, population increase and any kind of population dynamics are themselves something to be explained. They are not the ultimate explanation, because populations rise and fall and densities change in response to other particular phenomena. And it would seem that cultural phenomena would be responsible for much population change. For example, the kinds of crop production, techniques for handling disease, attitudes about birth control, abortion and infanticide and warfare all have an immense impact on population.

The deterministic theories so far explored have focused on factors external to culture itself. Economic and technological determinism, as well as the combination of these with geographical and demographic features known as cultural materialism, are yet other theories which depend upon specific cultural aspects. Let us now look first at technological determinism.

Technological determinism

Among anthropologists, Leslie White has no doubt been the most articulate protagonist of technological determinism. This position sees a direct correlation between the efficiency in use of energy and the general type of social organisation and in turn the ideology. That is, the level of technology is the determinant of the nature and character of the social organisation which in turn prescribes the nature of the ideological system.

Advocates point to the myriad of correlations one can make in these connections. Thus, as one type of example, hunting and gathering people seem to display a considerable uniformity in their social organisation. Hunters and gatherers, it is rightly pointed out, rely primarily on human muscle as the source of energy, supplementing this with fire and in some situations wind power and with the additional energy brought by the elasticity of sinews, etc., as in the bow. They are manufacturers of tools of stone, bone, ivory or wood, lacking any true metallurgy. They neither plant nor tend domesticated animals. In conjunction with such a technologically simple arrangement it is noted that several features of social organisation are ubiquitous: people are organised into what are referred to as bands – small face-to-face groups rarely having more than one hundred members. There is a lack of political organisation beyond this local group. Indeed, the social order has often been described in terms of negatives. Not only do they not have large populations, and extensive political integration, they also have no true government, no social classes or castes, no slavery or true warfare; ranks are ordinarily absent but if they occur are few in number; there is no specialisation of task, that is, no true division of labour and no system of markets. On the positive side we have small groups characterised by egalitarianism (at least amongst adult males), kin obligations and diffuse sanctions* as the techniques for preserving social order, the division of labour is based on sex and age alone, and goods are circulated largely through a system of reciprocity.

Other similar kinds of correlations can be made between a particular type of technology and social organisation for so-called horticultural, pastoral and agricultural societies. Yet when these various kinds of cultures are examined closely, I think we can come to only one conclusion: technology, like the physical environment, sets limits or conversely opens up new potentialities rather than directly and singly determining the specific nature of any culture. When we examine the hunting-gathering societies we discover they are not all of one piece. Surely they *tend* to follow the characteristics mentioned above, but these are only like so many broad strokes most roughly outlining this kind of culture. If technology were all we required to predict the nature of a culture, all cultures with the same technology should be the same in social organisation and ideology. Actually, the hunting-gathering societies we have been focusing on are highly divergent. One of the simplest technologies is associated with the Australian Aboriginal peoples who have evolved, on the base of a few simple principles, some of the most elaborate kinds of kinship organisation and exceedingly rich art forms, mythology and ceremonial systems. Within the parameters of hunting-gathering peoples possibly the Inuit or Eskimo have been the most sophisticated in creating a complex tool kit, yet their social organisation could hardly be any simpler.

When we compare hunter-gatherers with what presumably is a 'higher' level of technological efficiency – the horticulturalists and pastoralists – we encounter many more problems which seem inexplicable from a technological determinist point of view. The horticulturalists relying as they do on gardening and domesticated plant foods sometimes have social arrangements and ideological systems which are hardly distinguishable from hunter-gatherers.

---

* See p. 61, 'Is government universal to all human societies?'.

Other horticulturalists have systems which are indeed simpler than some hunter-gatherers. At the same time hoe gardeners in West Africa and simple horticulturalists in Central America (the Maya and Aztec) and in Peru developed hierarchical systems and other complex forms of social organisation all comparable to those identified with agrarian society, or what is referred to as civilisation, a system which presumably is based upon plough agriculture and other elaborate exploitations of energy. Pierre Clastres has suggested in particular reference to these archaic American Indian 'civilisations' that the fundamental changes, the real differences between them and any preceding simple Neolithic style cultures, is not technological at all but political. The Inca, for example, had an elaborate state organisation; their ancestors did not. Yet both shared a common 'Neolithic' style technology. Obviously then one would have difficulty accounting for this fundamental difference in social organisation by reference to some change in technology – some improvement in the level of energy exploitation.

Karl Wittfogel developed a technological determinist thesis concerning the origins of ancient civilisation in Egypt and Asia. These were for him 'hydraulic civilisations' which all commenced on the banks of great rivers. They were the source of elaborate artificial irrigation works which depended on the organisation of centralised mechanisms for control and hence engendered the development of the state, an accompanying urban life, social classes with their elites and literati and other amenities associated with archaic agrarian civilisation. This kind of culture is then a product of a particular kind of technology.

Paul Wheatley reviews the evidence for Wittfogel's claim and finds it wanting (1971, 292 ff). In China the large scale hydraulic works were intended mainly for transportation rather than agriculture. Furthermore they were not products of a centralised government except where they were specific military ventures. Rather, they were made and maintained by local or regional groups. For Mesopotamia Robert Adams has written that "... there is nothing to suggest that the rise of dynastic authority in northern Mesopotamia was linked to the administration requirements of a major canal system" (Kraeling and Adams, 1960, 281). The Mesopotamian walled city-state complex arose considerably before any large scale irrigation and must have therefore other causes. In the Andean region as well urban development occurred first and only some time later did major irrigation canals appear. Canals associated with the Nile were primarily built for transportation of stone for pyramid building and other public works or for draining swamps. Egyptian sources give no indication whatsoever of a role for irrigation canals in administration. If such technology were actually crucial for the creation of the Egyptian state one would expect otherwise. In more recent times, several different peoples living on the island of Luzon in the Philippines have had both highly decentralised anarchic social political structures and rather complex systems of rice irrigation. In this case of irrigation systems it is not that this mode of technology demands centralised hierarchical control in the form of state management. It is that it requires coordination of *some* kind – a coordination which can be achieved through a variety of different means.

Once again, then, we point to the extreme limitation of a technological determinist point of view. It can only outline in the broadest form certain constraints on culture and even then it is often in error or not at all helpful in enhancing our understanding. Technology too is affected by other aspects of culture and sometimes these can be more crucial than the technology in determining the direction of development.

Economic determinism and cultural materialism

For better or for worse, the name of Karl Marx is frequently associated with economic determinism. However, Marx seems to vary in his writings in the degree to which non-material forces are given importance. Throughout there is a consistent theme emphasising the central significance of social relations relating to property and of the technological base. Ideology he brings to the fore as having a 'feedback' value, but its causal role seems not to be recognised as of the same level and importance as that resulting from the economic and technological factors. Basic is the substructure or infrastructure which Berger and Luckmann have interpreted to mean 'human activity' (1976, 6). Nevertheless, one might also argue that to Marx the most important kind of human activity is 'work' and thus substructure at least emphasises the priority of the economic and technological, if it is not exactly identified with them. Superstructure (stressing the ideological realm) is a product of the infrastructure. As Marx himself may have altered his views on the causal role of economic-technological factors, it should also be noted that there has been little consensus among Marxist scholars regarding Marx's views on the subject. Some, including Lenin, have interpreted Marx as a solid economic determinist; others, pointing more to Marx's early writings, have taken a much less extreme position.

Marvin Harris among anthropologists has modified the Marxist approach and offered a 'cultural materialism' which considers the ultimate dynamic in any culture to be a combination of economic, technological, demographic and physical environmental forces. Social organisation and ideology are by-products of these. The major divergence of Harris from Marx is Harris's rejection of the dialectic process and acceptance, like Leslie White, of a mechanistic materialism by which change occurs as an automatic consequence of the several material forces.

A brief criticism of both Marx's and Harris's theories may be explicated by addressing a specific problem which has vexed scholars for over a century. This is the origin and development of the capitalist economic system. The following presentation is in most respects a kind of paraphrase of Max Weber's famous analysis and therefore underlines the inter-relationship of the ideological, economic and technological. It points to the priority of none of these, but rather the priority of the appearance of a particular ideology combined with a particular set of economic relationships and technology, all of which together allow for the appearance of a full-fledged modern capitalism.

Capitalism we may define as an economic system which is based on the principle of the individual ownership and control of the means of production and distribution. The most important property owners are 'capitalists' who provide the capital for operating enterprises and run them for the purpose of making a profit for themselves. The enterprise requires workers to produce the goods and make the profits. There is then a need for a large labour supply composed of individuals who are 'free' to work for wages for a chosen employer. The capitalist then pays the worker a certain amount for his labour in the form of wages and is interested in making a profit through such hired labour. Wage workers neither own nor control any significant property, nor are they tied as serfs to some landlord or as slaves to a master. In the latter sense then they are 'free' labour, but as essentially propertyless individuals they must somehow seek a livelihood, duly provided by the capitalist. In this system goods produced are sold in a market at prices established primarily by supply and demand.

This describes capitalism as it eventually became in the eighteenth century in western Europe and North America.* But capitalism as a profit-seeking venture by private entrepreneurs employing wage labourers is to be found in medieval towns and at other earlier times as well. Here it is not so much a system of production of goods as it is a trading of goods and a form of booty capitalism (such as Francis Drake). Under medieval conditions capitalist enterprise remained subordinate to the feudal system and was therefore an economic arrangement of secondary importance.

Ideologically, within the European cultural milieu there existed a 'work ethic', that is, the notion that everyone ought to work and that work is a good thing while laziness is sinful. However, it cannot be said that it was either prevalent or widespread. The great age of discovery, the invention of the printing press and, particularly, the Protestant Reformation, were major spurs to transforming European society from a feudalistic to a more completely capitalistic system. At the same time the 'work ethic' became more common.

In brief, the seventeenth century legatees of the teachings of John Calvin had evolved a particular ethic which was to become crucial to the evolution of modern capitalism. Essentially the theory developed from, but not to be confused with, the specific teachings of Calvin himself are as follows: God alone has ordained who is to be damned and who is to be saved. No one can know his own fate and no one, no matter what he does, can alter that predestined fate. It is the duty

---

* Particularly since the late nineteenth century capitalism has undergone significant changes. One important modification has been the enhanced popularity of the large scale joint stock company in which shares in the company are sold on the open market. The number of votes one has in determining company policy and the share in the profits is determined by the number of shares held. In effect the control of the organisation by a few immensely wealthy capitalists continues, yet at the same time those of more modest income, including wage workers, earn some of the profit through their purchase of a few shares. A second and related change has been the increasing control of capitalist enterprises by salaried managers who are not always coterminous with the big capitalist investors. A third major development has been the increasing interference of government in enterprise. Among other things there are capitalist corporations whose chief investor is the government. As a consequence of these and other changes, the capitalism of today is a much more complex and different entity than was the capitalism of 1867 when Marx completed the first volume of *Capital*.

of everyone, however, to behave as much like a true Christian as he
can, as if he were indeed one of the saved. That one did not act in
this way was a sign that he was one of the damned. Acting as if one
were one of the saved meant, among other things, that one worked;
this was how one glorified God and man's purpose on earth was to
glorify God. The earth in turn was given to mankind so that humans,
as stewards of the earth, would use it for the glory of God. Glorifying
God precludes wasteful living, profligacy, laziness and luxury. If one
worked and by God's grace did prosper, his accumulated wealth was
not to be put to wanton and frivolous living. One must be thrifty and
conserving not solely as a means to acquire wealth, but to demonstrate
that one loved God and respected his creation. A simple 'puritan' life
is therefore in order. Consequently, one who successfully
accumulated riches could not spend it in luxury and was left to
reinvest the wealth in the capitalistic enterprise. Here is the point
where the ideology is particularly significant to the capitalist system.
Capitalism requires financing for embarking on and continuing its
enterprises – to purchase machines, energy, labour and to expand
activity. This 'Protestant ethic' – work for the glorification of God,
accumulate wealth but invest it and do not waste it – becomes a
mechanism for financing capitalist enterprise. Puritans, Quakers and
others could devote themselves to hard work and build impressive
business enterprises. They were obliged to 'tend to business', to build
reputations for reliability, promptness, honesty and faithful
adherence to contracts, all of which lend confidence by the customer
or client in the business enterprise. The reinvestment of wealth
provided one technique by which an early capitalism could burgeon
and prosper. But we must not forget two points: one, capitalist
enterprise also expanded through investment from perhaps less
ethical sources and means, and, two, most people who worked, in
fact, were able to save nothing. In any case this Protestant ethic
provided a spirit of enterprise; it stimulated a motivation for action,
the extent to which it is a fiction is less germane.

In seventeenth century Europe capitalism possessed an ideology as
well as a form of organisation inherited from an earlier time. The third
major element of the system appeared in the latter part of the
eighteenth century and early decades of the nineteenth, and this was
a new technology. The industrial revolution, commencing about this
time, provided a new source of energy – steam – and new tools –

steam-driven engines – which could form the centre for factory-style mass production. Thus, to recapitulate, our point of view argues for the inter-relatedness of social organisation, technology and ideology. In the creation of modern capitalism it is suggested that the capitalist mode of organisation appeared first, followed by an ideology which stimulated growth of capitalist enterprise, but that modern capitalism as such appears as a major innovation when these facets are combined with the new technological mechanisms. Without any one of these major components modern capitalism would not arise. This is in contrast to normal Marxist and other economic/technological determinist theories which create capitalism as a mode of production with a given technology after which an ideology is created as a by-product to justify the system already created. Our argument is that ideology – the so-called superstructural aspect of culture – is actively involved in causation and the creation of culture.

Some other 'theories' about humankind

We have already encountered certain notions referred to as folk anthropology as they have been expressed in racial, geographical or technological determinism. In such thought it should be borne in mind there is rarely any of the consistency one would find with the more sophisticated expressions of such points of view. Thus a given 'man on the street' may well offer at the same time, and to account for the same set of facts, both a racial and a geographical explanation. Aside from those which have been mentioned, there are a number of other folk theories which seek to explain culture or major features within it, to which I believe it is appropriate to direct some attention. Some I would like to consider briefly here are: warfare is a natural and universal human activity; patriotism and love of country are natural and universal feelings; government is a universal and necessary form of organisation; competition is a dominant and universal human drive; human history is an automatic progression from simple and crude to complex and higher with the implication that the latter is always better than the former.

Is warfare natural?

All animals engage from time to time in intra-species fighting. Yet the deliberate attempt to kill an opponent seems to be a rare occurrence except among chimpanzees and the members of the human species.

Among other animals one or both combatants in a fight may be killed by accident, not by design or intent, although in cases of overcrowding it has been observed that fights will lead to killing. Ordinarily among animals a losing combatant in a fight runs away or performs an instinctive ritual act of submission which triggers an inhibiting reaction in the victor so that he no longer pursues his aggressive behaviour. Humans apparently lack any genetically programmed inhibitors that restrain a combatant from killing his opponent. What is controlled by instinctive ritual among animals is restrained by cultural regulation among humans. 'Thou shalt not kill' is a commandment of some degree of validity in every human community. It is not always effective. Not only do individuals in all human groups engage in hostilities in which there is a deliberate attempt to kill an opponent, but in every human society group endeavours of this kind occur as well. So it is argued warfare is a natural part of human behaviour. There have even been those who advocated it as a necessary inducement to any cultural group and development.

I would argue that warfare is not a half dozen men taking off to raid or engage an equivalent group in another camp. Inter-group hostilities are of varying kinds such that feuding and small raids can hardly be placed in the same category with warfare. Warfare possesses certain distinct characteristics which make it quantitatively and qualitatively different from other types of lethal combat. It is different in terms of both the aims and the organisation.

A war aims at conquest, that is, a warring group seeks to capture and control the lands, wealth and people of another group. The feuding and raiding which constitute the group hostilities in most human societies lack such aims. The intentions of the feud or raid are much more modest – to even a score, to steal livestock, to abduct women or, on rare occasions, to acquire territory. There is no motivation to subdue an opponent or absorb his group. In the feud once a member of one side has been killed or maimed a revenge attack can be expected in which a member of the guilty party will be killed or maimed. On the achievement of this mission the aggressors return home to await retaliation or a proposal for mediation.

The organisation of warfare is vastly more complex than other forms of group hostility. Wars are fought with armies and similar military forces. There are large numbers of men organised according to a chain of command and a division of labour. There are no democratic armies, since there are always some individuals who give orders to others who are expected to obey without question. Occasionally, an army falls into disarray because those at the top cannot agree, but armies are clearly distinguished by the fact that not only do those at the bottom do all the dirty work and face all the danger, but they take all the orders and give none at all. In addition, in a military force the chain of command is quite explicit and obvious to everyone. It is never ambiguous.

In feuding and raiding groups there is invariably no chain of command, or if it does exist it is a reflection of pre-established relations among the combatants. For example, deference may be made to one or two in a group because they are senior kinsmen or because they have a reputation for past success in disputes.

Not only are there commanders and the commanded in warfare, but some of the latter may be assigned to actual fighting, others to providing supplies to the fighters, some to repair of material, yet others to gathering intelligence, to reconnaissance or to tending to the wounded. And in each of these major categories there is invariably a further refinement in division of labour. Thus, the actual fighting force may be divided amongst those who are foot soldiers and those who are mounted or otherwise mobile, or those who employ projectile weapons and others who are maintained for hand-to-hand fighting.

Warfare requires at least a few semi- or full professionals and, for those who are neither, some kind of minimal training is involved. Warfare depends as well on tactics, that is, the organisation and plans for battle, the deployment of troops and the arrangement of the most efficient way in which to achieve a precise goal. Feuds and raids have no professionals and tactics are only minimally developed.

Because warfare entails the mobilisation of substantial numbers of men and supplies, it therefore demands a complex and large organisation which can mount and maintain it. This is why it is that true warfare appears only with the advent of the state. The state is a territorial association which claims sovereignty over a given place in space and all those residing within that area are subject to, and must submit to, the institution of authority ruling or governing that territory. That institution is the government. Criteria for membership within a state are determined by residence and by birth. Membership is ordinarily ascribed, although one may voluntarily apply to join if one immigrates and settles within the territory of the state. The state's apparatus of

government is to some degree centralised. The government functions
to the exclusion of other groups or individuals to execute existing
laws, legislate new ones, maintain 'order' and arbitrate conflict. The
government claims a monopoly on the legitimate use of violence
within the territory of the state. It further is composed of those who
represent special interest groups which tend to control the wealth and
power of the society.

The state through its government is a potentially predatory
organisation, jealously guarding its domain against outsiders and
seeking, as basically an organisation of power, to expand its influence
and control. Relations between states are ordinarily hostile. Peace is
mainly a balance of terror between approximate equals or, where
nations are not equal, the weaker become satellites of the stronger.
State and warfare are integrally inter-related wherein the state provides
the organisation and wealth (through taxation) necessary for the
pursuit of war and successful war in turn extends the power of the
state. Without a state organisation it seems unlikely that there would
be any other institution or arrangement within society to mount such
an enterprise. The record of anthropology demonstrates that stateless
societies engaged in feuding or raiding, not warfare.

In sum, warfare is not natural to humans. In the long sweep of history
it is, like the state with which it is bound, a very recent invention –
probably less than six thousand years old. If warfare is natural in any
way it is natural to nation-states – which represent only one kind of
human society.

Is love of country natural?
One of the continuing problems with folk statements is that they are
gross over-simplifications and hence distortions. They persistently
lump all kinds of diverse entities under one category. As we have seen,
in order to say that war is natural to humans we are forced to equate
it with a bar-room brawl. Now, in order to say that love of country,
or patriotism, is natural and universal among humans we are forced
to equate home and neighbourhood – that is one's face-to-face group
– with a country or nation-state. Or to say that government is universal
and essential in human society is to equate social order with government,
a misconception I shall consider below.

Clearly people do have strong attachments to home and neighbourhood. But once we pass beyond these people we know as kinsmen,

friends and neighbours – the normal primary or face-to-face group – such feelings must be manufactured by special interest groups. It is to the advantage of the nation to build an *esprit de corps* among its subjects, to have them all believe the nation is a 'home' and that therefore the health and well-being of the state are the health and well-being of the individual's home. In other words, the interests of the individual ought to be the interests of those who control the state. The essence of patriotism is the glorification of the interests of one particular state against others. And one is expected to glorify one state and not another, simply because one is subject to one and not the other.

As there is no true warfare without the state, so also there is no patriotism or love of nation or country without the state. Likewise patriotism is an integral part of the ideology of war. It becomes an honourable excuse to fight.

Is government universal to all human societies?

Above we alluded to the common practice of equating social order with government, but government is only one form of maintaining order in a group. Aside from government there exist various techniques for rule enforcement. One is what is referred to as religious sanction. Here a person obeys an injunction out of fear that if he does not he will be punished by some supernatural force either now or in some afterlife. Another class of sanctions includes such practices as gossip, ostracism, driving a person out of the community, duelling, feuding, vigilante-style action. These more diffuse kinds of sanctions are so-called because there is no monopolisation of the right to employ them by some select individual or small class, as one would find with legal sanctions, that is, governmental enforcement. Thus, gossip or ostracism may be undertaken by anyone; but only a policeman in our society can legitimately employ firearms to carry someone off to jail and that policeman is the agent of the government and the state. Only a few of all the human societies have governmental systems and even these supplement their law enforcement with diffuse and religious sanctions. The great majority of human societies have been stateless and governmentless. This does not mean that therefore chaos prevails, as was suggested by Thomas Hobbes. Order is imposed by different means, by the operation of various forms of diffuse and religious sanctions, and, positively, by the engendering of a sense of social solidarity and moral obligation to cooperate (*cf.* Barclay, 1982).

It is true that many of these people without government are hunter-gatherers who live in small bands and possess little or no property. Still there are a number of much larger populations of farmers and pastoralists which are equally without government. The Tonga in southern Zambia are an interesting example. They number several hundred thousand and are cattle herders and cultivators of corn, millet and sorghum. Tonga have no true chiefs or rulers, although they have influential persons who act as leaders. They perform as advisors, mediators and coordinators, but lack any authority to force others to obey them. A central mechanism of social control is the fact that any given individual is a member of a number of different groups, which in turn are part of a network of further obligations, so that any negative action against an individual or group resulting from one set of relationships has its counter restraining effect resulting from affiliation with other groups and individuals. Everyone has a close tie with his own matrilineal clan and that of his father. Clan ties are further extended through marriage alliances with other clans. Each clan has a set of other clans with which it maintains 'joking partnerships'. In these one should never become annoyed at the behaviour of his joking partner so in this way bonds aimed at avoiding hostility are extended to a large segment of the Tonga population. One belongs also to a neighbourhood which draws in additional people who are not otherwise part of one's social network. Additionally one establishes links through special brotherhood pacts and a system of loaning cattle to non-kinsmen. (By spreading one's cattle around one avoids a concentration of animals which in case of epidemic, raid or other catastrophe could destroy much of a person's capital investment.) By one connection or another a person ordinarily finds that effective restraining measures are built up to cover the important social relations one might have. The Tonga thus operated as a functioning social order without government. Their techniques of social control and building social networks made government a redundancy. Instead of centralised coercive authority there was a functioning anarchy (Barclay, 1982, 62; Colson, 1962).

While there are no large scale modern societies which operate without government, there are several interesting cases of large organisations and social movements which manage without any centralised coercive authority. Virginia Hine has described contemporary American social movements as "segmented polycephalous idea-based networks" or SPINs. A social movement such as the environmental movement or the black movement comprises a number of separate organisations which are all linked together like a fishnet without a central administration. What holds the various segments together and prevents disintegration is a wide range of 'horizontal linkages' and, most important of all, an ideological linkage: a deep commitment to a very few key and basic tenets which are shared by all in the movement. The horizontal linkages include overlapping of membership so that one person belongs to several groups within the whole movement. There is considerable interaction between leaders of the participating groups and leaders themselves may lead in one group and be ordinary members of another. Ritual activity such as demonstrations, conferences, rallies and marches provide further linkage. SPINs differ from centralised social systems in that each member segment is a self-sufficient entity which could persist even if all the others were destroyed. They have proved to be highly flexible and adaptable and, in sharp contrast to centralised hierarchies, they are egalitarian and emphasise personal inter-relationships (Hine, 1977, 19; also Barclay, 1982, 110-111).

The international postal organisation as well as continental railway systems exemplify other similar forms. The coordination of mail service between countries is achieved without a head, without a centralised administrative governing body. International postal service is a consequence of voluntary agreement by member nations to follow certain rules aimed at efficient passage of the mail across international boundaries. The specific regulations by which members are supposed to operate are established by a congress composed of delegates from member nations. Complaints about a specific national postal system are settled through binding mediation. The ultimate sanction against an offending member would appear to be boycott by other members.

The railway systems in North America and Europe at the international level function in a similar fashion. For North America there is an Association of American Railroads whose members include the major railways in the United States, Mexico and Canada. It is a voluntary organisation which sets standards for operation and particularly relating to the unencumbered passage of goods and passengers from one railroad line to another. A similar organisation exists for the entire Western Hemisphere and another is organised in Europe.

Must we always compete?

In the United States, Canada and western Europe – that is, the heartland of the capitalist world – a ubiquitous ideological statement emphasises the competitive nature of humans. This view was given an enormous boost by Darwin's theory of evolution and the derivative Social Darwinian notion that the evolutionary process of survival of the fittest was a justification for cut-throat competition.

Any survey of world cultures demonstrates clearly that the emphasis upon competitive rivalry which we find in our culture is absent or barely observable among others. The Pueblo Indians, especially the Hopi and Zuni, are classical examples of peoples who discourage competition between members and encourage cooperative group effort. The introduction of modern American schooling among them created several problems along these lines. Children were reluctant to strive for high grades in examinations; they did not want to excel over anyone else. The introduction of competitive sports was likewise not well received.

The so-called Northwest Coast Indians of North America are noted for their vigorous competition in the gift-giving ceremonies known as potlatches. In order to enhance one's prestige a person invites rivals to a feast at which goods are distributed to the guests and some may be deliberately destroyed. Later the guests reciprocate only with yet a bigger gift distribution and destruction of goods. The potlatches go back and forth between the competing parties as rivals seek to demonstrate their superiority and avoid being 'flattened' or outdone. Yet all this competition conceals the cooperation required to sponsor any potlatch, since the wherewithal for the feasting, distribution and destruction is provided by the cooperative effort of a sponsor's kinsmen. Similarly Ford or General Motors succeed in competitive rivalry because of the cooperation and coordination of their production staff.

It is sometimes said that those who are not competitive are precisely those who are not successful in the world. But success is a highly subjective idea that is culturally determined. Advocates of competition, as good materialists, see success as the accumulation of material wealth and the provision of physical comfort. Others would beg to disagree.

Competition is one human characteristic. It can be encouraged and made into a central feature of human behaviour or it can be downplayed so that it is hardly recognisable. At the same time competition is no more important, certainly no more natural, than is cooperation or conflict. Indeed cooperation and conflict seem to be universal features of human society and cooperation is an essential ingredient to the survival of any society. One cannot say the same for competition.

Cultural evolution and progress

A final example of folk anthropological generalisations which we might consider is the view that cultural progress is inevitable and automatic. Progress is a value judgement. We establish certain goals as desirable and the movement in the direction of those goals is therefore progress; any movement away is retrogression. Progress in popular lore in Western society has come to mean a movement from the simple to the complex and especially within the technological realm. Perhaps this idea has been considerably shaken in the past few decades and, therefore, is less widespread than it was forty or fifty years ago – before Hiroshima and Nagasaki. However, it continues to justify attention, particularly as it is often implicit in numerous evolutionary conceptions pertaining to cultural development.

Various theories of cultural evolution have been expounded over the years and most of them have been tied to the specific deterministic mechanisms which have been observed – such as the dynamic force of technology, of the physical environment, of population pressures or of economic forces. Earlier theories particularly were also married to the notion of progress: evolution was progress. Evolution was defined as a continual process of change characterised by ever-increasing complexity of forms and this in turn was deemed 'good' and, therefore, progressive. Stages of cultural evolution were delineated commencing with 'savagery', the simplest and most primitive form of culture when technology was limited to stone tools as the maximal form of sophistication, populations were dependent upon gathering wild plants and hunting animals and were constricted in size to tiny 'bands' of nomads of less than a hundred persons; religion was 'animistic' and shamans were the nearest thing to any kind of specialists in the society.

Depending upon your persuasion either technological or economic or population forces, or a combination of these, provoked eventual changes which catapulted society into a new and higher and more complex level of culture, the state of barbarism. Here certain plants and animals have become domesticated, productivity is therefore

enhanced and food resources more secure. Populations become larger
and sedentary village life can commence. Certain improvements in
stone technology presumably occur. Larger and more concentrated
populations create or lead to more complex forms of social
organisation – of larger tribes, of clans and lineages. Property in land
and livestock in this stage takes on greater significance and there are
at least marked differences which arise between groups in terms of
access to resources, so that if social classes are not readily discernible
we at least have a clear prefiguring of a society with social
stratification, one which sets the stage for the next, the third and
highest level of cultural evolution: civilisation.

Presumably this arises when the property issue provokes a division
into social classes: the propertied and propertyless. Simultaneously
this entails creation of a government and a state where the propertied
are also the rulers and the propertyless are the ruled. At the same time,
or slightly before, it is argued that technological changes occur.
Important among these are the harnessing of domestic animals for
traction (especially the plough is important here, but also wheeled
vehicles), the invention of metallurgy, development of complex schemes
of artificial irrigation and the invention of writing. Civilisation is
associated therefore with the appearance of an intellectual elite, a
literati, as well as urban centres – states and nations – and of
monotheistic universalistic religions.

Any hard, if not cynical, look at this kind of sequence would suggest
the optimistic nineteenth century European's view of the history of
the western world. Indeed, the chief model for the development of
this evolutionary sequence is in fact the European-western world.
Innumerable other societies never followed this sequence of changes.
In addition it has been found that characteristics allegedly integral to
one state of development are found amongst people who in every
other respect should be classed in another.

No one will deny that all human societies until ten thousand or so
years ago were roughly of the 'savage' type, nor will they deny that
the historical development of a large number of societies and especially
those with which Europeans have been most familiar have passed
again roughly through sequences as above defined. What, of course,
must be explicitly denied of any evolutionary theory is the following:
1. That societies *must* pass through these stages and in their proper
order.

2. That each of these stages is characterised by precise and fixed features as delineated above, that there is no room for variation.

3. That evolution works in a gradual and regular pace. (Rather it is probably more correct to say, as we did above in discussing the general problem of cultural change, that evolution moves by fits and starts. Periods of rapid change can occur in one location while others appear to remain static. At another time the static regions may experience rapid change.)

4. That the dynamism of the change can only be explained by 'materialist' forces such as population pressure, technology or economics and that beliefs, values and ideology are purely 'epiphenomenal'.

5. That evolution is to be equated with progress.

Cultural evolutionary theory also raises the question whether culture is to be treated as a class of phenomena or as one phenomenon. If it is a class of phenomena then it would be amenable to scientific generalisations since there would be a multiplicity of comparable cases – cultures – although the difficulties of drawing boundaries between cultures will be, to say the least, rather overwhelming. Further, the evidence which this 'specific evolution' approach yields clearly does not confirm any unilineal evolutionary process of all cultures passing through fixed stages and brings into question the general theory of cultural evolution. On the other hand, one may opt for a 'general evolutionary' position in which culture is seen as a single phenomenon; i.e., here one speaks of the evolution of culture in general. Now the data may appear to fit more correctly the evolutionary model, including the unilineal one, but one has a total universe of one, a unique case, which therefore makes scientific analysis impossible, since one cannot make generalisations and laws from one example alone.

If it is to be of any value, cultural evolution must be seen in broad and general terms. It must be relieved of the procrustean dogmas of stages of development and unilineality. As Julian Steward emphasised, cultural evolution is the theory that there are observable regularities in the process of cultural change and the task of the evolutionist is the empirical demonstration of what these regularities are.

One important regularity is a divergence of forms. Cultures having a common genetic origin become different from one another over time as each, among other things, adapts to varying external stimuli.

At the same time convergence is occasionally observable as different cultures become more similar, in part due to forces of diffusion. A third evolutionary process, and the one most stressed by the traditional evolutionists, is parallelism. Here different cultures, independently of influence from the others, change along similar or parallel lines as a response to similar influences. The independent and parallel development of Meso-American and Middle Eastern civilisations is one of the most common examples of this process. My emphasis here is that parallelism is obviously an important evolutionary mechanism, but it is only one and not a universal of all cultural change. Further, rather than the single or unilineal parallel development of all cultures hypothesised especially by earlier evolutionists, there are various lines or patterns of development. Some cultures apparently evolve along one line and others along another. So that, after Julian Steward, we can speak of multilineal rather than unilineal evolution.

Another observable regularity in cultural evolution is the tendency for more complex forms to appear out of simpler ones. Although this may be a major evolutionary theme, a lesser theme of the movement from complexity to simplicity must also be recognised. The evolution of writing is a case in point: alphabetic writing is more recent than pictographic representations, ideograms or syllabaries; it evolved out of these older forms and is much simpler than any of them.

Simpler forms also do not disappear in the face of new and more complex ones, and they may be more tenacious and adaptive. If we turn for a moment to biological evolution, perhaps there is some kind of message in the fact that cockroaches, for example, have been around for millions of years readily and easily adapting to a variety of different conditions, while 'higher' more complex forms appear to fall by the wayside after a short presence on earth.

Complexity in human culture is not unequivocally good or progressive. It is the more complex societies which have produced war, slavery, genocide, death camps, human sacrifice and more benign forms of human oppression. Social equality and 'democracy' are best discovered amongst the 'simple savages'.

Undoubtedly largely because of the cultural milieu in which we live, most observers have looked at the historical record from an evolutionary, if not downright progressive, perspective. But perhaps an anti-evolutionary or anti-progressive view is equally tenable. Consider the following: one, the immensely long history of human-like creatures on this planet, extending back three to four million years. Second, compare to this the sophistication of technology over this period. For the first 3,985,000 years that technology was extremely simple. The last 15,000 years have witnessed a veritable technological 'revolution' by comparison. Third, observe the difference in population increments and densities. During the first 3,985,000 years there were probably less than ten million hominids at any one time, but in 15,000 years the number has sky-rocketed to over five billion.

How would some Olympian observer looking down on us from Sirius interpret this process? This apparent fact that in the last 15,000 years, or four-tenths of one percent of the total time span, 'human' culture has undergone the most immense change, like a culture gone wild, and at the same time population has jumped accordingly. Applied to the life of a forty year old person, it would be like spending ninety-nine and six-tenths percent of his life in reasonably stable conditions and the last four-tenths of one percent of the time, or two months, in gigantic and revolutionary transformations. Similar changes in the human organism with which we are familiar today are diagnosed as cancers.

Such a grotesque picture is certain to please the purveyors of gloom and doom. I do not, however, believe doomsayers need be hastily shrugged off. Nevertheless, I would conclude this essay with two criticisms of the above tale which will permit us to end on a more positive note. First, if we limit the story to our own species, *Homo sapiens*, only the dramatic effect disappears since we would be looking at more in the neighbourhood of the last hundred thousand years, not four million. The changes would then appear more gradual and less spectacular. Finally, a theme in this work has been that human beings are intelligent creatures who possess the capacity to assess situations and make choices. They have, then, a degree of freedom and control and are not locked into some inevitable destiny wrought by uncontrollable forces. Humans are unique creatures who, faced with diagnoses and predictions, are able to alter their behaviour and modify conditions so as the invalidate such prognostications. Hopefully they may be sufficiently literate so as to read the present handwriting on the wall.

Bibliography

Harold B. Barclay, *The Role of the Horse in Man's Culture* (J.A. Allen, London, 1980).

Harold B. Barclay, *People Without Government: an anthropology of anarchy* (Kahn & Averill, London, 1990).

Peter Berger and Thomas Luckmann, *The Social Construction of Reality: a treatise on the sociology of knowledge* (Anchor Doubleday, Garden City, New York, 1967).

Mary Boyce, *A Persian Stronghold of Zoroastrianism* (Oxford, 1977).

Elizabeth Colson, *The Plateau Tonga of Northern Rhodesia: social and religious studies* (Manchester University Press, 1962).

Henri DeLubac, *The Unmarxian Socialist: a study of Proudhon* (Sheed & Ward, 1948).

Marvin Harris, *The Rise of Anthropological Theory* (Crowell, New York, 1963).

Virginia Hine, 'The Basic Paradigm of a Future Socio-Cultural System' in *World Issues* II, 1977.

A.L. Kroeber, *Anthropology* (Harcourt Brace, New York, 1948).

Paul Wheatley, *The Pivot of the Four Quarters* (Edinburgh University Press, 1971).

Karl H. Wittfogel, *Oriental Despotism* (Yale University Press, 1957).

3.

Do Anarchic Polities have a Message?

Some general characteristics of anarchic polities

Almost all hunting and gathering societies of which we have any record are egalitarian and anarchic, having no government or state. A small minority – typically those of the north-west Coast of America and of northern California – are rank societies which nevertheless frequently lack any governmental system. Among horticulturalists the extent of egalitarian and anarchic polities is still widespread, but less so than among hunter-gatherers. On the other hand, probably a minority of pastoral societies, and hardly any agricultural ones, fall into this category. Among the latter, societies are characterised by stratification and the state.

The egalitarian quality of any polity, anarchy included, it must be remembered, is to be seen within the context of same sex and general age or generation. True sexual equality is a rarity and societies which approach it are, like the Ifugao or Dayaks, more often than not those which have a bilateral kinship system. With it there is a lack of differentiation or preference regarding relatives through either parent; there is an equality, or an approximate equality, in terms of inheritance through either parent and by members of either sex. Husband and wife will tend to bring to the new household equal amounts of property. This bilateral situation usually sets the stage for relatively equal participation within the economic sphere (e.g. Ifugao, Inuit, Samek). Matriliny sometimes appears inferior to bilaterality in its ability to provide the most secure basis for a relative sexual equality. This is because in it males are often motivated to neutralise the principle of inheritance through females by asserting their own dominance.

Anarchy correlates with 'folk' or *gemeinschaftlich* characteristics. It is easiest where the population of the maximal effective social group is small – probably up to two hundred individuals. In it 'face-to-face' relations prevail and thus the typical diffuse sanctions of gossip, ostracism and the like can operate most effectively. Anarchy is easiest where the population is homogeneous and undifferentiated. Among other things this means there is only a minimal division of labour and specialisation of task. Such a situation where people are much the same reduces or minimises the opportunities for differences of opinion, sharp cleavages and conflict, and maximises what people have in common so that even if there is disagreement there is still immense pressure to conform and keep the system going. Numerous bonds of commonality bind the dissident to the group and prevent total alienation.

Some may interpret these conditions as rigidly curtailing freedom. Freedom, it may be said, is measured by the number of choices open to an individual. And there are obviously fewer choices open to members of these small scale societies. But perhaps we should question how much less freedom exists in such societies if all the members are unaware of a greater number of alternatives and if the same few alternatives are available to all. How, indeed, would such societies compare to those more 'modern' ones in which there are presumably so many more choices, but in fact they are not freely available to everyone?

While it may be said that anarchy occurs most frequently in a small group situation and is probably easier to perpetuate in this condition, this is not to say that it is impossible in a modern more complex context. Rather it is more correct to say that it is not very probable. Yet we do have examples of anarchic polities among peoples such as the Tiv, Lugbara, Nuer and Tonga, numbering in the hundreds of thousands and with fairly dense populations, often over a hundred people to the square mile. Such social orders may be achieved through a segmentary lineage system which has certain parallels to the anarchist notion of federalism. Or, as among the Tonga and some East African pastoralists, large populations may be integrated by a more complex arrangement which affiliates the individual with a number of cross-cutting and bisecting groups so as to extend his or her social ties over a wide area. In other words, individuals and groups constitute a multitude of interconnected loci, which produce the integration of a large social entity, but without any actual centralised coordination.

Even within Western civilisation we have cases of large acephalous organisations. SPINs, the railway system and the international postal service have been mentioned above (pages 63-64).

It is somewhat ironic that certain defenders of a powerful national state are at the same time advocates of an economy which not only lacks a centralised control at the international level but also has none at the national level. The old liberal capitalist notion that an economy is, or ought to be, a self-regulating system controlled only by the demands of a free market, is in its essence an anarchist notion. However, it no longer remains one when it becomes a guise for exploiting and oppressing others. In any case, these several examples are what Bohannan has referred to as 'multicentric' power systems.

It is clear that large, relatively complex social systems or relationships can function efficiently in an anarchic fashion. It is, however, noticeable that none of the ethnographic cases available suggest the operation of anarchy where there are major urban agglomerations. Except for the brief Spanish and Ukrainian experiments, wherever anarchy obtains it is in a rural context. Still, if anarchy can function in a densely populated rural area, there is again the possibility that it could operate in cities as well.

The fact that there are few anarchic polities among complex social structures may mean that the centralised state has appeared to be a more practicable mechanism by which to maintain social relations in such a milieu. It may also mean that certain individuals with power are able to anaesthetise the populace into believing their authority is indispensable and that life is easier by abdicating responsibility to them. The ruled are instilled with the notion that government knows best; it is the most efficient vehicle for providing services to the community, while the ordinary folks are neither qualified nor capable. Like any successful institution, government also prospers by inculcating its necessity in the populace. Once power has been accumulated into a few hands it is more difficult to get rid of it. It has a savage appetite and the habit of cancer, ever expanding and enlarging. There has been over the decades a gradual erosion of self-help and voluntary co-operative institutions in our society, an erosion which has favoured an increasing encroachment of government into the lives of all. This is not only to be criticised as a threat to liberty, but it is equally a threat to the everyday practice of voluntary cooperation, of self-reliance and mutual aid between 'natural' groups in society.

Even if we set aside the real possibility that the masses have been drugged by those who achieve power, we might consider that people's weighting of human values have too often been such that they elect security over freedom, order over liberty and efficiency over individuality. The plain fact is that anarchy requires work, responsibility and a big gamble. Especially today, the majority of people are content to abdicate responsibility to government – perhaps because they are too lazy and because they have been happily mesmerised by those in

power; perhaps, also, because their self-confidence has been under-
mined by the powerful.

Cultural florescence and anarchy

In *Nationalism and Culture* Rudolf Rocker explored the hypothesis
that wherever there is a state there is an inhibition of human cultural
development and, correlatively, wherever political integration is weak
and limited to small groups cultural 'progress' occurs. By culture
Rocker refers to the various arts: architecture, painting, music,
literature, philosophy. Unfortunately he fails to make any systematic
analysis of cultural contents or to disengage the subject from the most
subjective level. He makes only personal judgements about the value
of Roman literature or of Greek sculpture, for example. Obviously
this is an area in which objectivity could hardly be achieved. An
equally serious problem is that Rocker seems to view with approval
the ancient Greek city state, the early Spanish commune and the small
principalities of seventeenth and eighteenth century Europe. It is not
clear, then, whether he is critical of the state or critical only of big
states. Whatever the case might be, the argument that cultural
florescence is suffocated by the state is a fascinating question, but one
replete with too many pitfalls to be answered in any convincing way.

To pursue properly Rocker's question we would require a more
precise conceptualisation of the state and above all we would need an
objective technique by which evaluation of art forms in different
cultures could be made. This formidable task I have no intention of
pursuing. A.L. Kroeber in *Configurations of Culture Growth* attempted
something of this sort. He made no evaluations of art forms, but used
the names of noted persons as indices for plotting the rise and decline
of the several arts and sciences in the major civilisations of the world.

His aim was to determine regularities in the growth of intellectual
and aesthetic endeavours in the course of time and from one major
civilisation to another. His technique is by no means beyond
reproach. And in his conclusions, unlike others such as Spengler or
Toynbee, Kroeber finds no grand pattern or patterns, no historical
universals. He finds no significant inter-relationships between the
climaxes of particular configurations, whether these be in the natural
sciences, philosophy or arts. Nor are there connections between
culmination in a given art and a total cultural climax. The crest of a
scientific wave may come before, with or after that of a literary wave,

and so on. Cultures often have great climaxes in some arts and sciences and none at all in others. More directly as a response to Rocker, Kroeber finds configurations and their culminations are not particularly related to such factors as the lack or extent of political integrations. Both Kroeber and Rocker are only concerned with literate civilisations. One wonders how Rocker, for example, would have looked upon the cultural development among the anarchic polities discussed in this essay, compared to others which have states.

For one thing, we have noted that in such governmentless societies there are nevertheless numerous oppressive features which would seem to inhibit free creative expression. What is more, the atmosphere of freedom in and of itself is insufficient for cultural florescence. The free do not create in a vacuum. It is sometimes pointed out that the Australian aboriginal hunter has much time to think and create, but the end product is not that impressive. Aside from freedom, one requires the appropriate stimulation. The accumulation of knowledge is a certain spur to that stimulation. As one gathers more data one's understanding is eventually enhanced. New connections and relationships are seen; greater insight is achieved and new hunches or intuitions flash into one's mind. The specialisation of task is a major factor in producing a creative atmosphere, because there is the opportunity for a number of individuals interested in the same specific problem to exchange ideas, work together and so inspire each other. Such inspiration is accelerated as one has easy and free communications around the world with others of like concerns. Now *historically*, specialisation of task in the division of labour – the building up of a community of scholars or artists – is invariably associated with some urban development and the creation of a leisured class. This suggests, then, a stratified society which has little place for anarchy.

No one can deny that some degree of personal freedom and individuality is essential for innovation and cultural florescence. But, contrary to Rocker, it seems that cross cultural analysis and history tell us that humans can be creative under quite dissimilar circumstances. The quantity of freedom which may be essential is highly variable. Certainly no one can argue that the various anarchic polities will have greater developments in the arts simply because they have no state.

Techniques for maintaining order

Freedom and individuality as enunciated in the anarchist movement
are European, if not bourgeois, values which grew out of the
Protestant Reformation and have roots further back in Greek cultural
tradition. Most of the people with which we have dealt maintain an
anarchic system and display certain individualist traits but do not
commonly explicate philosophical thoughts on freedom. As a matter
of fact, we may well be valuing these peoples for reasons important
to us but not to them (*cf.* Colson, 1974, 62).*

A society may be free of governors, policemen, jails and law – the
whole apparatus of government – but this by no means guarantees it
will be a free and egalitarian society. The reliance of anarchic polities
upon diffuse and religious sanctions may lead to tyranny. The taunts,
the gossip, the ostracism and the physical violence which form part
of such sanctions often appear unyielding, unforgiving and cruel. And
as we know from our small town life, there is little place of refuge from
such sanctions so long as one desires to remain within the community.
Diffuse sanctions are often difficult to control and can readily get out
of hand, as with the vigilante committees of the Old West. What is
more, they may be a force of conservatism, stupidity and intolerance.
Nevertheless, we who dwell in state dominated societies not only must
submit to diffuse sanctions but also the overwhelming power of the
state as well. And in our age of sophisticated technology – particularly
in the realms of communication, transportation and electronic
surveillance – the state has access to an incredibly awesome power.
The real tyrannies in this world have been and are state tyrannies.

Anarchic techniques for maintaining order stress self-help and
self-regulation, which from the point of view of an American or
European may sometimes appear like a perpetual resort to violence
in the form of the feud. Lee has addressed the question of relative
homicide rates amongst San as compared to the United States and
other areas. He calculated the San rate at 20.3 per 100,000 person
years. In the United States there are 9.2 homicides per 100,000
population while a study of 23 Ugandan peoples showed a range of

---

* In their drive to build modern nation-states and ape the Europeans, Africa's
political elites are eager to bury the archaic anarchic elements, or to convert
them into the idiom of democratic statism. Old African anarchic decentralism
becomes in their hands an example of some ancient African tradition of
democratic government and communalism.

between 1.1 and 11.6 per 100,000 with a mode of four to six. The US figures would be far higher if its medical facilities were as rudimentary as those of the San. Moreover, it is noted that many automobile and other accidents in the United States are intentionally homicides but are not counted as such. Far more important is the number murdered in warfare and none are counted in the homicide rate. Consequently Lee revises the American figures and estimates the proper rate in the United States to be about 100 per 100,000. He also figures British, French and German numbers would be equally as large. However, I would suspect that his estimates are too high. Nevertheless, his conclusions are valid, namely that San homicide rates are probably quite a bit less than those in the United States and that while the state may be effective in reducing certain kinds of violence, such as individual fights, it creates new forms, such as war (Lee, 398-399).

Our survey of anarchic polities shows how widespread is the presumed reliance upon the feud, which can be so wasteful of life in its apparent senseless murder and mayhem. What is more, the feud provokes a prolonged state of anxiety and psychological turmoil. However, it is well to bear in mind that the destruction of the feud in an anarchic polity is hardly likely to approach that of the warfare which is conducted between states. While there are no available comparative figures, there is at least one basic difference between feuding and the nature of war which helps substantiate this conclusion. That is, feuds aim at evening a score. The operating thesis is an eye for an eye. They do not aim at annihilation of an enemy or unconditional surrender of the opponent. Often, once someone has been injured in a feud, the fighting stops. At least active peace negotiations will be initiated because of the priority of the maintenance of group harmony. It is essential in any conflict to restore that harmony as soon as possible. Litigation of any kind is not aimed at finding blame for blame's sake, but in satisfying disputants and bringing peace. This entails a central role for third party mediators or go-betweens. These respected men consult with opposing sides until some compromise can be reached. The success of such ventures depends on the ability of the mediator and on the sense of moral obligation to play the game on the part of the parties involved.

Elizabeth Colson believes, however, that it is not so much actual feuding but fear of provoking a feud that is an important mechanism

of social control in acephalous societies. She refers to recent reviews
made independently by E. Adamson Hoebel and Sally Falk Moore
which conclude that there is not a great deal of evidence for feuding
as such, but a great deal of evidence for fear of the feud. In anarchic
polities everyone becomes very much aware of the potential
consequences of rash behaviour. Each person learns the need for
self-restraint: "some people live in what appears to be a Rousseauian
paradise because they take a Hobbesian view of the situation: they
walk softly because they believe it necessary not to offend others
whom they regard as dangerous" (Colson, 1974, 37). "There *is* 'peace
in the feud' as Gluckman has said, but it is a peace based on the
prevention of the first act rather than on the force which leads to the
final settlement" (Colson, 1974, 43).

It has been suggested that people in anarchic polities have less to
quarrel about because there is less property and much homogeneity and
equality. But perhaps again restraint is important because of the fear of
consequences, so that there appears to be less quarrelling (Colson, 1974,
43).

An obligation to play the game is elemental to the functioning of any
anarchic polity. And, of course, it is readily enforced by fear of diffuse
and religious sanctions. Nevertheless, those who are used to living in
a society governed by policemen and legal sanctions often fail to
appreciate the significance of the sense of obligation to play the game
as a motivating force for social order even within their own society.
We must not forget that in all human societies most members chose
to follow the rules because they want to and because they believe in
them. They would resist any attempt to lead them into non-conformity.
In any society, sanctions of whatever kind are for the tiny minority.
Were all law enforcement to be removed tomorrow there would
probably be an initial burst of crime, but after the novelty wore off it
would dissipate. At the same time, the vast majority would not be
involved, but would go about its business as usual. To hold, as some
apparently do, that were the law to be removed there would occur
some momentous explosion of brutish and murderous behaviour
among all the populace is, in the first place, grossly to overestimate
the present power of the police. More importantly, it is grossly to
underestimate the years of conditioning about right and wrong to
which all have been exposed and the power of the internalised censor
or conscience.

In those cases where traditional techniques for social control have been removed suddenly or greatly relaxed, two consequences are noteworthy. One is the extent to which voluntary mutual aid spontaneously appears and spreads – people begin helping each other. The other consequence is the opposite response – the one the 'law and order' supporters would predict. That is, there is rioting, looting and mayhem. But the reason for this reaction is not because there is no police to keep order. The reason is suggested by the kinds of people who engage in such behaviour. These people are definitely not the members of society who have prospered from it, nor are they the ones in positions of prestige, power and influence. On the contrary, they are always from the ranks of the disadvantaged and frustrated. And the revolt – which is what it is – is an attempt at catharsis, to relieve pent-up aggression and hostility generated by a system perceived to be oppressive (whether it is 'in fact' oppressive is beside the point; it is seen to be such and that is what counts).

It is an error to think of humans as 'naturally' good; it is equally erroneous to condemn them as monsters. And radicals, of all people, should appreciate the extent to which people are conformists.

Some criticise anarchy because its only cement is something of the order of moral obligation or voluntary cooperation. But democracy, too, ultimately works in part because of the same cement. And it works best where the cement is the strongest. That is, democracy ultimately does not operate only because of the presence of a police force. The free elections and two-party system could never survive if they depended upon the army and the police to enforce them. They survive because participants have a belief in the system and a feeling of obligation to play according to the rules. Hocart has said that government depends on "spontaneous and incessant goodwill ... Without it governments would collapse" (129).

De la Boetie, Machiavelli and Spooner among others would add, however, that in any system of government submission is induced by fear and fraud. In *The Politics of Obedience: the Discourse of Voluntary Servitude* Etienne de la Boetie devotes himself entirely to the question of why people submit to rulers. He makes the following points:
1) People submit because they are born serfs and are reared as such.
2) People are tricked into servitude by the provision of feasts and circuses by their masters and because they are mystified by ritual practices and religious dogmas which aim to hide the vileness of rulers

and imbue reverence and adoration as well as servility.

3) The 'mainspring' of domination is not physical force so much as
it is a chain effect: the ruler has five or six who are his confidants and
under his control; they in turn control six hundred and these in their
turn control six thousand. "The consequence of all this is fatal indeed.
And whoever is pleased to unwind the skein will observe that not the
six thousand but a hundred thousand, and even millions, cling to the
tyrant by this cord to which they are tied. According to Homer, Jupiter
boasts of being able to draw to himself all the gods when be pulls a
chain" (78).

Also suggestive of why people obey is Lysander Spooner's
classification of "ostensible supporters of a constitution": knaves,
dupes and those who see the evil of government but do not know how
to get rid of it or do not wish to gamble their personal interests in
attempting to do so.

In anarchy there is no such delusion for there is a priority placed
upon individual freedom which is absent in democracy. Democracy
– granted its concern for liberty and individualism – nevertheless, like
any other system of rule, puts its ultimate priority in the preservation
of the state. When in a democracy one group threatens to withdraw
– to secede – there is always the final recourse to a 'war measures' act
to compel compliance and suppress 'rebellion'. To summarise, order
in the anarchic polity is founded in diffuse sanctions. It is maintained
through self-help, self-regulation and self-restraint and these devices
are channelled by fear as well as by the motivation to make the system
work and to play the game with a minimum of friction.

Group decision-making

Part of the democratic myth is the sanctity of majority vote. That every
so many years each voter goes to the polls and chooses a leader by
majority, and the secret ballot, is the most sacred ritual of democrats.
Anarchists have argued that this is no true indication of liberty.
Rather, again as de la Boetie might have observed, the election of
rulers by majority vote is a subterfuge which helps individuals to
believe that they control the situation. The voter, in fact, chooses from
a pre-selected group and invariably there is no choice between
contrasting ideologies. The difference between major parties – those
that have a chance of victory – in any western country today is no
greater than the difference between factions within the Communist

Party in the Soviet Union or China. No one could seriously argue that there is any ideological or any other enduring traditional philosophical contrast between the major parties in the United States or in Canada. In addition electors might be reminded that they are selecting individuals to do a task for them and they have no guarantee that it will be carried out as they desired. Above all, this job in its essence is one of forcing obedience. Electing men to public office is like being given a limited choice of your oppressors.

Quite often election by majority does not even occur. A candidate for office is elected because he or she has more votes than any single other candidate and actually receives much less than a majority of the votes cast. In addition, the number of people who don't vote – the silent majority – is never taken into account. Presumably a goodly proportion of the non-voters are not particularly enamoured of any candidate. In 1976 in one American state, Nevada, voters were given the alternative in the Presidential election of marking an X beside 'none of the above' – the nearest thing to an anarchist vote. Slightly less than 3% of those who voted made this choice. In addition, 40-50% never bothered to vote.

We frequently hear the refrain 'if you don't vote you have no right to complain'. Such an argument makes the false assumption that an election provides for real choices. And, of course, it falsely assumes the legitimacy of the process itself: that an individual is required to delegate authority to an arbitrarily chosen few, or that an individual is required to elect his or her own jailers.

Above all, there is the fundamental moral question about the sanctity of the majority. Democracy, in its advocacy of majority rule, attempts to provide an alternative to the rule of one or of a few, but it often replaces that kind of dictatorship by one of the majority or, most commonly, of the plurality. It assumes that right or wrong, that morality, is determined by a majority of those who bother to vote. Ibsen's *Enemy of the People* is a vivid dramatisation of some of the consequences of relying upon majorities. Yet even aside from the fact that minorities may know better, or have right on their side, there remains the truth that the majority compels the minority to conform.

The anarchic polities which we have considered, as well as anarchist theoreticians, have stressed an alternative decision-making device – that of consensus. An issue is argued out until everyone agrees or acquiesces to a given solution or, in lieu of such agreement, the matter

is set aside, usually to be taken up at a later date. The Society of
Friends (Quakers) in our own cultural tradition has long practised
this technique as a means of conducting business. Decisions depend
upon coming to a sense of the meeting: a point when there is no
further expressed opposition to a plan of action.

There are many arguments against this approach. It invariably
entails a considerable amount of talk. Indeed, a member of an
anarchist intentional community once said that the main product of
his group was talk. But there is nothing more human than talk and as
long as people engage in it they will not engage in violence.
Consensual politics is most commonly criticised on the grounds that
business could well be hamstrung by a stubborn minority. This is
sometimes the case, but this can also occur in a democratic legislature,
which can be as inefficient and time consuming. If one wants an
efficient system one would probably do best to appoint a select
committee of technocrats to plan and expedite legislation, but this
would not be a free society; it would be Orwell's 1984 world.

A more creditable criticism of consensual politics derives from the
manner in which it tends to work out in actuality. First, consensual
politics is effective with small groups since it depends upon full and
open discussion of issues in a kind of face-to-face relationship.
Secondly, in practice there is no equal participation by everyone.
Rather the people of influence in the community impress their
opinions upon others so that individuals fall in line and at least come
to a tacit agreement. Indeed the people of influence in a community
may often confer ahead of time and agree to a position for public
consumption. Anyone 'holding out' and preventing consensus is
ordinarily 'prevailed upon' by influential individuals to see the 'error'
of his or her ways. All these kinds of political manoeuverings are
equally as common in democratic and other politics. The advantage
of a consensual system is that ideally it is morally superior to others
in protecting minority rights. Clearly it can become an unwieldy and
coercive instrument. Anarchists themselves, in their implementation
of communes and collectives, have often found it necessary to resort
to the democratic system of majority vote.

An alternative to consensus is decision by lot. Election of ministers
and other church officers among the various Anabaptist sects has
often been by this process, in the belief that one must avoid the
possibilities of strife which might come from the partisan politics of

majority vote elections, and leave the decision up to God who presumably expresses himself in the lot. Election by lot assumes, however, a high degree of group homogeneity, or at least some kind of control over who are to be the potential candidates. One can imagine what would occur if, in the United States, one of the candidates in a lot was a Communist and he was in fact selected.

The search for a decision-making process which is both moral and efficient must yet continue. At least in the smallest more homogeneous group, or in one committed to the priority of group harmony, the consensus technique seems more advantageous.

Types of leaders in anarchic polities

From a review of anarchic polities, different kinds of leadership and attitudes towards leadership emerge. In most cases leadership is looked on positively and to become a 'chief' is an aspiration of the many. There are, however, a minority of societies in which it is considered impolite or unethical to strive for paramountcy in any way. Leadership roles are de-emphasised and are not quite approved. Yet, whatever the attitude, leadership patterns in any group do emerge and we may note at least four different types amongst anarchic polities:

1) The Big Man;
2) The Technician;
3) The Holy Man;
4) The Old Man.

The Big Man is the one who acquires a central position of influence in the community and a following of clients as a result of his wealth, his ability to persuade and to orate and occasionally because of his physical prowess. Here is the Yurok or north-west coast Indian 'chief'. Here also is the Big Man of New Guinea.

The Technician achieves paramountcy especially in hunter-gathering societies. Thus one who is a good hunter collects around him a following which is willing to do his bidding and be fed, such as among Athabascan Indian bands of the Canadian sub-Arctic or among the Inuit. Modifications of this role are found among the San and Pygmies. And the Samek headman is a master technician for a pastoral people.

The Holy Man, through some religious ideology, is accepted as a prestigious person to whom all voluntarily defer, particularly as a mediator of disputes. Here we have the Nuer leopard-skin chief or the maraboutic families and lineages of the Imazighen. Also of a slightly different order is the Inuit shaman who acts not so much as mediator but as a manipulator of people, often for his own ends (a role which mixes the Holy Man and Big Man concepts).

The Old Man is the leading member of the community simply by being the senior male member of the kin group. While the Big Man and the Technician are more frequently achieved statuses, and the Holy Man may be either an achieved or an ascribed one, that of the Old Man is ascribed, although even here there may be the slight element of achievement. Thus some elders may be more pre-eminent because of ability in speech, having more wives, more wealth, more sons or knowledge of ceremony and esoteric doctrine. The Old Man syndrome is characteristic of Australians and particularly of the African horticultural societies (Tiv, Lugbara, Konkomba, Tallensi, etc.). Some segmentary patrilineal systems combine the Old Man and the Holy Man syndromes, as with the Arab Bedouin.

Earlier it was noted that authority might be considered as rational or irrational. In connection with the above four kinds of leadership it would appear that only the Technician represents a rational form. The others also have clear elements of rationality, but have at the same time irrational or arbitrary qualities. This is most true of the role of the Old Man.

In Max Weber's classification of types of authority, both Big Men and Holy Men fall into the 'charismatic' type, while Old Men combine the gerontocratic and patriarchal attributes of 'traditional' authority. Weber does not really make provision for the Technician (Weber, 324 ff).

Conservative theory holds that the tribute offered the ruler is fully reciprocated by the services of the ruler to the people. This argument has been challenged by persons from a broad spectrum of ideologies, from the democrats to anarchists. Indeed, it seems only the height of self-delusion to contend that all forms of rulership are reciprocal. How could the relationship between an ancient Egyptian peasant and a pharaoh conceivably be seen as a reciprocal one? Where is the reciprocity in the enormous wealth which is yearly handed over to the British royal family and the positive services it presumably offers? Does not every ruler acquire special privilege and an essentially non-reciprocal relationship with clients or subjects? Indeed, we may, with Pierre Clastres, say that another way of defining rule is as a non-reciprocal relationship. The ruler is the paramount example of that status.

Henry Orenstein discusses two types of asymmetrical reciprocity: the centripetal and centrifugal. The first is the leader as servant and is best exemplified in Pierre Clastres' analysis of South American Indian chiefs. Here it will be recalled the chief's advantage is seen as a breaking of the fundamental law of social relationships – reciprocity – resulting in a suspicion of power and a desire to contain it. Paradoxically, the chief is contained by his own asymmetrical reciprocity: his excess of wives places him in perpetual debt to the community, so that he must forever be a servant of the people and can never affirm coercive power as a true ruler. This conception of the centripetal 'chief' works against governmental and state organisations.

Orenstein thoroughly confuses the issue when he suggests that centripetal leaders and rulers include such widely variant persons as a South American Indian chief, a Roman emperor and the elected official in a democracy. If this were in fact true, it would make the concept of centripetality useless and meaningless. The centripetal leader is correctly a leader within the most pristine of anarchic polities: he is a servant whose clientele may, if they choose, ignore him with impunity. What democratic elected official or Roman emperor could ever be ignored? Even the command of the justice of the peace must be obeyed on pain of punishment.

In centrifugality the ruler or leader maintains a type of relationship which can command obedience and services. What we have called the Big Man and the Holy Man ordinarily have centrifugal relationships. It is out of this kind of context that we have the creation of the despot and of government. But before exploring this issue further, I would like to suggest that perhaps some types of leaders in anarchic polities are neither centripetal nor centrifugal. Perhaps leaders of certain polities only engage in the ordinary reciprocal relations of everyday people. Consider leadership among the Pygmies. Here it seems to be only of a temporary sort, highly amorphous and 'multicentric', always surrounded by a reluctance to lead or to be aggressive. There seems to be no special advantage to be derived from leadership and the leader is not indebted to his people. The Pygmy leader appears to embody the best anarchic ideal, because he minimises leadership characteristics and retains normal reciprocal relationships with others.

On the origins of the state

As we have seen from our survey of anarchic polities, the seeds of
tyranny and government are readily observable in the performance of
many leaders. The Tiv, Lugbara and other African polities, as well as
the Australians, exemplify the potential tyranny of Old Men. The
patriarchal system, it might be argued, does have a certain rationality
in that it is the elders who have lived the longest and so presumably
have acquired the most experience in living as well as having had the
greatest opportunity to learn the wisdom of the ancestors. But it is
irrational in that it assumes that all those in 'elder' status are
automatically always superior.

By its nature the old man syndrome *alone* cannot perpetuate an elite
power group as a dynasty. A man assumes power as an older person
and retains it for a few short years, at which time he must yield to new
persons who were his subordinates. Indeed, in an age-graded society,
such as the Tiv, a man assumes leadership for a short span of a decade,
when he must retire to inactivity and now find himself in a social
setting where those who were his subordinates are now leaders.
Another reason patriarchy in this anarchic setting may not lead to
government *per se* is that the entire system is intimately attached to
kinship. Patriarchs or elders are always grandfathers of some kind.
One is not obligated to obey those one does not address with a
paternal type kin term.

The germ of state development might find a more fertile location in the
role of the Big Man. In New Guinea this leader acquires a body of clients
which he is able, in some cases, to command. Mair has contended
that the foundation of a state could be in this development by a leader
of a dependent and loyal body of supporters. Slightly different is the
individual among the Inuit who is able to lord it over a community
by his own physical force or use of dreaded supernatural powers.

With the Big Man, anarchy can then degenerate into tyranny. What
sometimes occurs may be seen as an abortive attempt to introduce a
governmental-state system. It is invariably a failure because there is a
definite ambivalence within the community towards authority, so that
if established it regularly inspires rebellion and the Big Man who tries
to be the bully is most often murdered. Thus the situation returns to
an acephalous or more anarchic condition. In addition there is no
precedent for establishing a succession pattern so as to perpetuate a
dynasty. It is also clear the New Guinean and other systems do not

develop permanent states out of their Big Man leadership pattern because there is no adequate economic, technological or organisational base. The New Guinea Big Man is limited by the productive capability of his dependents and this is inhibited by lack of a more complex technology. Nor can one expect to control extensive territories with the available very simple methods of communication and transportation. At the same time the Big Man's power is maintained and extended only through a network of personal contacts. There is no organisation of loyal bureaucrats to sustain the realm. The difference between king and Big Man is fundamental: kings receive tribute and submission; Big Men must rely on support. "Rather than being a stage in the evolution of government, the state, or rather the monarchy, is but a point on one end of a spectrum whose other end is stateless societies containing only big men" (Schneider, 207).

Leaders among the Ifugao represent yet another type of Big Man. In their role as go-betweens they have the legitimate right to command contending parties to mediate, on threat of violence. Government then, in a most limited sense, has been instituted.

Clastres believes that the state cannot rise out of the 'chiefly' role, but this view requires some modification. First, it is least likely to arise in those cases which clearly fit the qualifications of centripetal leadership. Here it does not arise because the community is vigilant in restraining the chief. Nevertheless the Anuak village chief exemplifies a leader of this sort who under certain circumstances can apparently expand his authority. Secondly, the sort of anarchic leadership characterised by the Pygmies is even less conducive to state development. Not only does the community frown upon any vigorous exercise of authority, but individuals have been conditioned to avoid the aggressive affirmation of leadership. Thirdly, the state as a permanent institution has difficulty in appearing in those centrifugal systems such as in New Guinea for reasons we have just enumerated. On the other hand, a governmental institution may be more likely to appear in connection with certain kinds of mediator roles, as among the Ifugao. But, also significant in this regard are the roles of Holy Men. To be sure, Clastres sees these as different from his centripetal style chiefs and recognises the possible emergence of government in the role of prophet among the Guarani Indians in South America.

Hocart has argued that the earliest government-like functions were assumed by ritual specialists, some of whom in the course of time become fully-fledged rulers of states as part of the general process of increasing specialisation in the division of labour. In Marxist theory power derives primarily, if not exclusively, from control of the means of production and distribution of wealth – that is, from economic factors. Yet it is evident that power derived from knowledge – and usually 'religious' style knowledge – is often highly significant, at least in the social dynamics of small societies. The Australian leader derives his power by his control of esoteric ceremonial knowledge, the Inuit shaman by his controlling of curing techniques and the manipulation of the dark arts. The Nuer leopard-skin chief has the power of the curse, as do the elders and rainmakers among the Lugbara. The foundation and legitimacy of the Anuak chief's role is in its ritual and supernatural significance. Economic factors are hardly the only sources of power. Indeed we see this in modern society, where the capitalist owner does not wield total power. Rather technicians and other specialists command it as well, not because of their economic wealth but because of their knowledge. For the anarchic polities we have looked at, it is clear that the functionaries with knowledge are often entitled to invoke sanctions which at least border on the legal. As was just noted above, the Ifugao case, as well as the Nuer and Lugbara, suggest that the germs of government often first appear when the mediator role is transformed into a judiciary one, which also has ancillary police-like powers. A separate and distinct police force would presumably be a later development.

Countless authors agree that the state arises with social differentiation and increasing social complexity. Such views often implicitly argue that the state becomes a necessity as an integrative device. This is apparently the thesis of Wittfogel, who in his hydraulic theory of state origin correlates the rise of the state with the development of extensive irrigation systems. The latter necessitate coordination and the state is the grand coordinator. Much data has been assembled to demonstrate that complex social arrangements, whether irrigation works (e.g. the Ifugao) or the international postal system, are coordinated in lieu of the state. In addition, of course, the fact that the state does appear constantly in connection with highly complex social arrangements does not mean that it *must* occur, nor that it *ought* to appear.

Oppenheimer, among others, argued that the state originates out of conquest. The expansion of one group so as to conquer another gives rise to an apparatus aimed at maintaining domination. The major drawback to a conquest theory of state origin is that before a group embarks on the war path it has already become a state. The examples Oppenheimer presents are of social entities which were states when they commenced expansion.

Anarchic polities engage in hostilities which are best not confused with warfare, but rather should be called feuding. This is because, among other things, true warfare entails the organisation of armies with a chain of command and with the intent of subjugating an enemy and occupying his territory. For those societies we have investigated above, it is apparent that some have the germs of governmental organisations, but they engage in neither real warfare nor in conquest. In other words, some kind of governmental structure is perhaps an essential prerequisite to engaging in the true warfare necessary for conquest. One requires at least the rudiments of an administrative system to order new subjects about. At the same time the truth of Oppenheimer's theory is that pursuit of warfare and conquest invigorates a burgeoning state and helps elaborate the administrative hierarchy. State and conquest are best seen as mutually interdependent phenomena which 'feed back' on each other.

Intrasocial conflict affords another explanation of state development. The Marxist theory of class conflict is the most notable of such theories. It argues that where there is an economically dominant class there is a state and where there is no state there is no class system. Marxist theory identifies property accumulation with the evolution of the state. And such a correlation was made as well by anarchists. Kropotkin and Bakunin both believed the abolition of capitalism – private property – was a prerequisite to the building of an anarchist society. Proudhon, however, saw that private property – which is used to intimidate, exploit and subdue others – was in truth 'theft' and incompatible with anarchy, but individual property not so employed was not. Our survey of anarchic polities seems to substantiate Proudhon's view. The societies we have encountered recognise individual ownership of important resources and where, as in New Guinea, those resources are frequently used as devices to create a body of dependents we have 'Big Men' who take on a more tyrannical character than leaders in other anarchic polities who do not seek to acquire economic control over others.

The Marxists Barry Hindiss and Paul Hirst have claimed that with "the primitive and advanced communist modes of production" there

is no state because there are no social classes.* Such a view ignores
the bureaucratic-managerial elite as a class, thus unveiling one of the
weaknesses of Marxist theory. That is, the bureaucrats as non-property
holders are not seen as a social class and so are not seen as worthy of
further consideration. Yet they are nevertheless a potent social force
which perpetuates the division of society into the powerful and the
powerless. Such observations are not intended as a demonstration of
the falsity of a class theory of state origin. Rather they are intended to
question the absoluteness and dogmatism with which this theory is
sometimes enunciated. Neither government nor social class can be
developed to any extent without the other also appearing. The case
of ancient Iceland demonstrates that social classes can exist without
the state, but not for long. Governmental functions restricted to the
local headman as a kind of proto-state require no class of rulers, but
a full-blown state with government applied to extensive areas and
large populations does. And those who control and own the society's
wealth will certainly be part of the ruling class.

Often leaders in stateless societies have been transformed into
governmental officials as a consequence of contact with already
existing nation-states. People bordering on China's northern frontier
no doubt created states as a consequence of the role of their notables
as intermediaries, especially in the trading activity. Among Afghan
tribes men of influence assume the role of chief liaison agent between
their own people and a neighbouring state. Increasingly they come to
accumulate the trappings of governmental authority themselves and
so help create states. Similarly, European colonial powers in the
process of their territorial aggrandisement on contact with people in
stateless societies recognised certain individuals as 'chiefs' of the
'tribe' and insured for them formalised power positions. Thus,
stateless societies are either transformed into states themselves or are
absorbed into existing states.

All the relevant case material presented here concerns societies
which for the most part exhibit only rudimentary forms of government
and social class. They suggest, then, that in what might be seen as the

---

* Modern anarchists face a dilemma if they propose the abolition and
prohibition of private property, in that in order to do so they would seem to
require an institution suspiciously like a state to ensure its abolition and to
ensure that it remained abolished.

earliest phases of state development there are alternate paths of social change. Ronald Cohen has written that "there is no clear-cut or simple set of causal statements that explains the phenomenon of state formation ... The formation of states is a funnel-like progression of interactions in which a variety of pre-state systems responding to different determinants of change are forced by otherwise unresolvable conflicts to choose additional and more complex levels of political hierarchy". Once this is achieved there occurs a convergence of forms towards the early state (142). Yet clearly involved in the beginnings of state formation is an inter-dependent development of government and social class tied to an economy which is able to provide the means to sustain an elite class. Hierarchy, submission and tribute are characteristics of any fully-developed state and these cannot properly bloom until society has the proper wherewithal, economic and otherwise, 'to deliver the goods'.

Even more fundamental ingredients for state formation are the individual will to power and the creation of a division between leaders and led. From these basic elements we have noted several different paths for further elaboration in the direction of the state. Thus leaders, in their capacity as mediators, may acquire authority to impose legal sanctions, first possibly in a restricted sense and eventually broadening the realm of control. Other kinds of leaders may build a loyal body of dependents who in turn legitimise the use of force by the leader. In these cases wealth and knowledge are important bases for establishing one's credit as a ruler. Men's associations may assume governmental functions and if these are in the hands of age grades we might expect the system to be more democratic. In some instances we have encountered, such as New Guinea, the seed of statism has been planted but has never truly germinated. In others, such as the Tiv or the Ibo, there is only the most limited growth – there is an anomalous condition with the barest rudiments of the state. State development may be a subtle and insidious process by which the distinction between leader and led is transformed into one between ruler and ruled. In looking at anarchic polities one can only discern at best the very beginnings of this development – the prelude and first lines of the first act in the drama.

I suspect that one of the most common scenarios for state (and class) development commences in the initial anarchic polity with the existence of some kind of 'Big Man' who was at one and the same

time a recognised mediator of disputes, an impressive manipulator of
supernatural forces and above all a central figure in a redistribution
system in which he held impressive feasts for and made loans to a
considerable number of individuals who consequently became his
dependents and retainers. As the Big Man thus enhanced his wealth
and power, trade increases, labour specialisation becomes more
widespread and populations increase, particularly as a consequence
of improved productivity. The social order then becomes more
heterogeneous, composed of groups with increasingly divergent
interests and outlooks, so that inter-group conflict becomes more
common and more important. Thus, the mediator and mystagogue
roles of the 'Big Man' are augmented. He can turn some of his
dependents and retainers into armed guards and enforcers,
abandoning his role as mediator for that of arbitrator-ruler. Thus
human societies which once were all egalitarian, acephalous and
anarchic entities are transformed into hierarchic, authoritarian states.
At the same time some of the more favoured henchmen of the 'Big
Man', through their own machinations and especially through being
able to establish themselves as centres of lesser redistribution systems,
are able to increase their own wealth and power so that they are
increasingly differentiated from the rest of society. An elite class of
controllers of wealth and power with the 'Big Man' at the top is
created over a subordinate class of producers of wealth.

Finally, Pierre Clastres has made an interesting observation on the
phenomenon of state formation, although he might slightly overstate
the case. He maintains that the shift from hunting-gathering to
Neolithic agriculture is not a decisive revolutionary change since old
patterns of social organisation were not altered that radically. In
addition the Middle American states were dependent upon an agricultural
system of the same technical level as the anarchic 'savages' of the
forest. The real revolution is the rise of the state and of 'hierarchical
authority', not economic transformation. "Perhaps one must acknowledge
that the infrastructure is the political, and the superstructure is the
economic" (171). Thus is Marx turned on his head.

Does anarchy have a future or is history a one-way street?
Whether anarchy has any future requires us first to consider how to
dispense with the state which now prevails everywhere. Secondly, we
may inquire into the general pattern of historic and cultural trends

regarding state development and the prospects for a libertarian age from that vantage point.

Three general techniques for abolishing the state and government have been most commonly proposed by anarchists. One advocates undermining the state by the creation of a multitude of voluntary associations whose functioning will make the state superfluous. Another favours violent revolutionary overthrow. A third approach is non-violent direct action, which includes such a syndicalist technique as the labour strike. Why anarchists avoid electoral politics should be obvious from what has already been said about anarchism. But in short anarchists have no faith in such a technique because they do not believe one can defeat an enemy by joining him.

The attempt to make the state superfluous was popular amongst the early nineteenth century anarchists. Proudhon hoped to initiate at least the decline of the French state by a proliferation of mutual associations which would loan money interest-free. Several Americans, including Josiah Warren, had similar ideas, particularly entailing monetary reform and mutualism which were seen as paths to the free society. Much later Gustav Landauer wrote: "The state is not something which can be destroyed by a revolution, but it is a condition, a certain relationship between human beings, a mode of behaviour. We destroy it by contracting other relationships, by behaving differently."

Another approach along these same lines is the intentional community. Indeed, Josiah Warren saw his communities as demonstration experiments which people would be able to observe, be impressed by and copy. Always the anarchic intentional community is an attempt to 'contract other relationships', to 'behave differently' and find alternatives to the state.

But many who seek to 'build the new within the shell of the old' are essentially indifferent to the ultimate fate of the state. For many who have participated in intentional communities the motivation is a personal one: of finding immediately a different, and presumably better, life for themselves and their families. They are unconcerned about its potential consequences upon the state, or at least that is of very secondary significance. Yet some who are interested in building mutual associations in part as devices to undermine the state, simultaneously pronounce the obvious anarchist truth that the state is an institution which will not voluntarily abdicate its power. Those in power would never come to see themselves as superfluous and, as they have done on countless prior occasions, they will act to suppress any perceived threat to their positions. The state in a modern capitalist society, as in Canada and the United States, may readily tolerate, even encourage, credit unions and cooperatives and any number of other mutualist voluntary associations. This support would soon turn to suppression if such movements became a threat to the banking and corporate interests of the country. In addition, such organisations readily tend to become 'establishment' oriented. Rather than having a modifying effect upon their environment, it is the environment which modifies them in a more conservative direction. Cooperatives, for example, are notorious for becoming as large, as bureaucratic and nearly as capitalistic as the more traditional organisations. Do not misunderstand. I am all in favour of mutual associations and of Landauer's call to contract other relationships. However, such techniques are extremely limited and it is hard to see how, by themselves, they can produce a transformation to a stateless society because, by one means or another, no state will permit it to happen.

Another course of action suggested by anarchists is violent overthrow of the state. We have seen the use of violence as a diffuse sanction amongst various anarchic polities. Yet this seems inconsistent with an ideological commitment to the doctrines of anarchism. Violence is the technique of the state and the ultimate form of coercion. Those who adopt it as a means cannot help but be tainted by its use. A main reason for the anarchist rejection of participation in the governmental process is that it will have a corrupting effect upon individuals, turning them into politicians seeking power and personal glory. No less can be the case for those who take up violence in the attempt to find justice. Yet the strongest arguments against anarchist resort to violence is that any effective violence necessitates a military structure, which must clearly be the most anti-anarchist form of organisation conceivable. Can one imagine an army organised on anarchist principles of voluntary cooperation and consensus? The implications and logical consequences of pacifism would seem to be anarchism. The view of some Quakers that there can be a non-violent state or government is self-contradictory since the state is, by definition, based upon violence. Otherwise it is not a state and must be a polity based on other than legal sanctions. Conversely anarchists, who would be the first to recognise this inherent nature of the state, have often justified war and in this sense have sought to use statist methods to abolish the state.

Bakunin expected the revolutionary zeal of the masses to be spurred on by a group of selfless devotees who had no care for themselves or their own glory. They were to be a body of strong, educated personalities who would not seek to lead, master or direct the masses. Instead they would learn what the people desired, articulate it and, with their broader knowledge and understanding, better be able to aid in pushing the revolution towards the goals set by the masses. This vanguard would be an anonymous and invisible body blended into the background. Thus, in part, is the justification for Bakunin's romance with secret conspiratorial groups. The revolutionary vanguard Bakunin saw was to be drawn from the large number of 'declassed intellectuals' and middle-class students, "children of peasants or the lower middle-class, the children of unimportant civil servants and bankrupt gentry" – any who have no chance of pursuing a career or position (Lehning, 189). Lenin was influenced by this Bakuninist idea, but as a 'realist' his vanguard had lost all the high-minded altruism which Bakunin, in his romantic and naive way, held to be imperative. In contrast to the fascists, whose elite is a vanguard of heroes, Bakunin's is a vanguard of saints.

In general any proposal to build the barricades is today a purely romantic notion which is strategically stupid. Military technology has become so sophisticated and expensive that only governments can invest in it and support it. A guerrilla army would find itself faced with overwhelming odds and its only hope would be to incite the military to join the revolution – a most unlikely event.

The third technique, that of non-violent direct action, is the viable alternative to violent revolution. It requires much self-discipline and patience, demanding that one be satisfied with minuscule successes and slow transformation. Certainly this, coupled with the movement to build voluntary mutualist associations, is the only approach having much feasibility. Yet no prospects can be promising, particularly when one looks at the general trend of history.

The anarchic polities we have discussed in this essay are largely phenomena of the past. Anarchies have been transformed into subject entities by colonialist states and then gobbled up by third world nations. Their old social structure has been modified so as to accommodate to the proper functioning of the modern state. The lineage elder is now a 'chief' who may call upon the local constabulary for aid; the mediator becomes the judge who now commands. 'Indigenous' anarchies are a dying breed, an endangered species. This process seems to support the contention that the main thrust of history is towards the creation of states and authoritarian forms. It is a movement from decentralisation to centralisation, from small to big. While we may cite case after case of the growth of states out of an earlier anarchy and have noted several germs of statism in our examples, the evidence of anarchy evolving out of the state is next to non-existent. Indeed, not only is the trend towards state organisation, but it is towards bigger and fewer states enveloping the world.

Recently Robert Carniero showed how the number of polities (of all kinds) in the world has, since at least 1000BC, continually declined "and not only has there been a decrease in the number of autonomous political units in the world; the tendency has accelerated. It is quite clear that the rate of decrease in the number of independent political units between AD500 and AD1976 was much greater than it was between 1000BC and AD500" (Carniero, 214). Overall, during the three thousand year period from 1000BC to the present, he estimates the decline has been from several hundred thousand polities to 157 in 1976. We may cavil that the latter figure is too small since it includes only the world's nation-states and fails to take into account the fact that in many parts of the world there are cultural groups which persist as autonomous political entities despite the claim of some nation to the territory. Still the decline is dramatic and, what is more, it would be yet greater for anarchic polities since we must assume that a high proportion of societies in 1000BC were of this type while few, if any, are today.

Carniero attempts to project the approximate time we must anticipate the creation of a single world state. He arrives at, not 1984 but about 2300. Such projections can be discounted as rather fanciful, but what cannot be overlooked is the clear major trend towards fewer and bigger states.

The usual argument against anarchy runs something like this: people are not perfect; they require constraints; the bad need to be confined in jails. The moment one institutes a free society based on voluntary cooperation there will arise people who will seek to take advantage of the situation and accumulate power themselves. Further, as societies become larger and more dense in population and more heterogeneous, the problems of order and decision-making become too complex to be left to consensual techniques and diffuse sanctions. So from this vantage point as well there are pressures to centralise, institutionalise and formalise authority patterns.

Anarchist theoreticians have long warned of the dangers entailed in the assumption of power even by the most idealistic. Bakunin particularly attacked Marxism along these lines. He was rightly somewhat more than suspicious of the 'dictatorship of the proletariat' and correctly predicted that it could be "nothing else but despotic rule over the toiling masses by a new, numerically small aristocracy of genuine or sham scientists" (Maximoff, 287). Later W. Machajski, a Polish participant in the Bolshevik Revolution, came to similar conclusions about the Soviet Union for, as he saw it, the proletarian revolution had been transformed into a dictatorship of the party hacks. Arguments along these lines were further expanded by Max Nomad.

In 1911 Roberto Michels published his *Political Parties* in which he expounded the 'iron law of oligarchy'. This law states that all organisations develop in the direction of increasing authoritarianism, bureaucratic and oligarchic rule. Whoever says organisation says oligarchy. To demonstrate his thesis Michels analysed the history of the several European political parties. Later Seymour Lipset and others sought to refine Michels' interpretation by studying a labour union, the International Typographers Union, which did not seem to follow the pattern of the inevitable move towards oligarchic rule. From this investigation Lipset and his cohorts suggested some conditions which might preclude a bureaucratic and authoritarian development. Interestingly enough they entail little an anarchist theoretician might not have told him: small units, a variety of autonomous local voluntary associations, several interest groups none of which can control or monopolise power, no great differences in socio-economic status and general state of economic security for all, an educated population and one which shows a high degree of participation in communal affairs, a high sense of group solidarity, and leaders who are not given much salary or status difference. In other words, 'chiefs' must be servants – impotent coordinators in a centripetal relationship. I would also suspect that a conscious will of the membership to preserve a free society is no small factor in this process.

Perhaps the Industrial Workers of the World is another example which deviates from Michels' law, and for reasons similar to those Lipset found for the typographers. Yet while we may scout about looking for exceptions, the prevailing directions seem in accord with the 'iron law of oligarchy'. Thus, among labour unions, for the one or two which have avoided this direction there are a hundred which have not.

Aside from the general trend for complex organisations to develop internal changes which produce oligarchy, there is yet another type of observable trend which commences with voluntary associations and ends as well in an authoritarian structure. This pattern was pointed out by Bert Buzan in a paper on 'Voluntary Cooperation and Social Democracy: The Case of Twentieth Century Neo-Populism' delivered at the International Symposium on Anarchism (1980). Buzan reviews the history of the farmer-populist movement in the United States between 1880 and 1920 and notes that it originated with various apolitical voluntary mutual aid associations. The most important of these were cooperatives aimed at marketing farm products. These, however, met with the concerted opposition of vested economic interests. Thus railroads refused to carry their goods; land and buildings were not available for sale or rent for grain elevators and warehouses. Because of this sabotaging by capitalist enterprises the members turned increasingly to electoral politics, spawning the People's Party, Farmer-Labour Party and Non-Partisan League. In their devotion to seeking reform through government they moved away from voluntary cooperation to depend more on formal legislation. At the same time, of course, the cooperative associations themselves became large, bureaucratic and political lobbying groups (in line with Michels' predictions). Thus in addition to an internal dynamic which pushes an organisation towards oligarchy, there is the external process which propels individuals to abandon those voluntary associations they have in favour of dependence upon bureaucratic and governmental ones.

Now the question arises, perhaps the movement towards centralised oligarchy is only part of a long term historical process of oscillation between decentralisation and centralisation. Yet it is difficult to find examples of trends towards decentralisation – at least of a libertarian nature. Periods of so-called cultural or organisational decay in history may suggest this sort of trend. But what trends do occur in these situations is the creation of a number of petty despotisms out of one which had existed before. Decentralisation is not accompanied by freedom. The revolutions and revolts of history and the decay of social systems have invariably entailed the replacement of one kind of despotism by another. Or what is a process of decay of one polity is the basis for the creation of another, so that, for example, the appearance of Clovis's Frankish kingdom and of the Umayyad caliphate follow on the heels of the decline of Rome. Power abhors a vacuum. A few South American Indian societies referred to above appear to have become anarchic as a consequence of a general process of tribal disintegration. Yet this situation seems uncommon and is limited to extremely tiny polities. Those few societies, such as the Pygmies, which provide not the slightest hint of embarking upon a course towards a governmental or state organisation are also small and highly homogeneous without any specialisation of task. They exemplify that rarity wherein members have been diligent in restraining the forces of authority and wherein events have been such that members have not been detracted from that noble pursuit. Perhaps one must conclude that the main thrust of history is towards centralised states with occasional minor 'pulsations' of reaction – slight and temporary reversals or people running off on alternate paths. Perhaps also the last decade and a half has experienced a feeble resurgence of this kind in parts of the western world. Thus there is not only the enormous increase in the number of communal experiments, but there is the movement of individuals 'back to the land', to simplification of life and revolt against the establishment. More important has been the appearance of mass social movements based upon 'segmented poly-cephalous idea-based networks'. Unfortunately these several activities remain largely confined to the offspring of middle-class white society alienated from the values of their parents.

Back in 1963 Paul Goodman, in *People or Personnel,* pointed out how centralisation has now made industry inefficient, creating excessive congestion and problems of transportation and communication. With the diffusion of electric power it is possible and more sensible to decentralise production. This theme has been reaffirmed continually. Schumacher harks back to Kropotkin and Goodman, noting how 'small is beautiful'. Recognition that small group operations and decentralisation can be more productive and obviously more humane is coupled today with some growing recognition of the inefficiency and alienating effects of large impersonal centralised organisations. Recently Marshall McLuhan offered a mixed prediction for the 1980s. It was mixed in the sense that part foresees greater decentralisation by the expanded use of the home computer, television, telephone and other 'electric software', but it is not necessarily a prediction of individual liberation in that with this expansion of new technology McLuhan sees as a further disappearance of personal identity – the disembodiment of individuals and a new form of government by 'pollstergeists'.

In spite of the various 'recognitions', hopes and predictions, and in spite of the movements into the intentional community or out to the land, states continue to become more powerful and centralisation goes on essentially unabated. Certain biological species are reputed to have become so specialised that they cannot adapt to changed environmental conditions and so become extinct. Perhaps there is a parallel to the potential fate of those social systems which become so utterly complex and overburdened with top-down administration that they collapse. Hopefully out of the remains might arise, like a Phoenix, a simplified and decentralised system. But would this only generate its own tyranny?

Humans as intelligent beings have some control over their own destiny. As they increase their knowledge and understanding in the world, and particularly of their own behaviour, they should better be able to manipulate their environment and modify their social order so as to make life more agreeable. Yet knowledge and understanding are intimately tied up with values and priorities of values. They are circumscribed as well by the apparent fact that humans appear to be rather conservative beasts willing to change from the known to the unknown and the untried only in the direst emergency. Therefore, while presently there may be a greater realisation of the possibility of a '1984 world', other priorities than freedom and individuality may have precedence. Further, this possibility is not perceived as an immediate and overwhelming threat. When we consider the numbers who persist in such a simple thing as cigarette smoking in spite of overwhelming evidence of its relation to cancer, how can we expect people to be concerned about such more abstract and apparently less obvious matters as threats to personal freedom?

Not only is anarchy unlikely to be achieved because of the improbability of dispensing with the state, but even given the abolition of that institution, the prospect for subsequent modes of organisation remaining decentralised, autonomous and free is as doubtful as the likelihood of the participants being truly dedicated to 'freedom, equality and justice for all'.

The kind of free society which might be more durable and resistant to corruption would be one in which each person and group was involved in a complex web of mutual relations such that each bond within the web would act as a counterbalancing force to every other. In this way every participant would be constrained and unable to expand his or her realm at the expense of any other.

Proudhon saw human societies as being engaged in a struggle between 'freedom' (anarchy) and 'authority'. But he was imbued with the rather naive nineteenth century notion of progress and optimism. He had faith in the eventual victory of the forces of freedom. An Australian group (the Sydney Libertarians) has, one might say, adapted Proudhon to the latter part of the twentieth century. They envisage a perpetual struggle between 'freedom' and 'authority', neither one of which will be annihilated.

It appears, indeed, that we are left with a politics of perpetual protest. There cannot be any point at which those dedicated to liberty can sit back in security and assume the world is in peace, harmony and freedom. That a truly free society may never be attained – or, if achieved, would have the most tenuous life – is clearly no excuse to abandon the struggle. If we resign ourselves to what is, there would hardly be much point in living. And even if anarchy were to be achieved, eternal vigilance would be the bare minimum price for even a modicum of success. Despite what the international anthem of the revolutionary class might say, there is no final battle. The battle is forever!*

---

* Perhaps this might be called the anarcho-cynicalist point of view.

Bibliography

Etienne de la Boetie, *The Politics of Obedience* (Free Life Editions, New York, 1975).

Paul Bohannan, *Social Anthropology* (Holt, Rinehart & Winston, 1963).

Robert L. Carniero, 'Political Expansion as an Expression of the Principle of Competitive Exclusion' in *Origins of the State* edited by Ronald Cohen and Elman Service (Philadelphia, 1978).

Ronald Cohen, 'State Foundations: A Controlled Comparison' in *Origins of the State* edited by Ronald Cohen and Elman Service (Philadelphia, 1978).

Pierre Clastres, *Society Against the State* (Urizen, New York, 1977).

Elizabeth Colson, *Tradition and Contract: the problem of order* (Aldine, Chicago, 1974).

Paul Goodman, *People or Personnel* (Random House, New York, 1964).

Barry Hindes and Paul Hirst, *Pre-Capitalist Modes of Production* (Routledge & Kegan Paul, 1975).

Virginia Hine, 'The Basic Paradigm of a Future Socio-Cultural System' in *World Issues* (No. II, 1977).

A.M. Hocart, *Kings and Councillors* (Chicago, 1970).

A.L. Kroeber, *Configurations of Culture Growth* (University of California, 1944).

Gustav Landauer, *For Socialism* (Telos, St Louis, 1978).

Richard B. Lee, *The Kung San: men, women and work in a foraging society* (Cambridge University, 1979).

Arthur Lehning, *Michael Bakunin: Selected Works* (Grove Press, 1973).

Seymour Lipset, Martin Trow and James Coleman, *Union Democracy* (Doubleday, 1956).

Lucy Mair, *Primitive Government* (Penguin, 1962).

G.P. Maximoff, *The Political Philosophy of Bakunin: Scientific Anarchism* (Free Press, 1953).

Roberto Michels, *Political Parties* (Dover, 1959).

Max Nomad, *Aspects of Revolt* (Noonday Press, 1959).

Franz Oppenheimer, *The State* (Bobbs-Merrill, 1912).

Henry Orenstein, 'Asymmetrical Reciprocity: a contribution to the theory of political legitimacy' in *Current Anthropology* (No. XXI, 1980).

P.J. Proudhon, *The General Idea of the Revolution in the Nineteenth Century* (Freedom Press, London, 1923).

Rudolf Rocker, *Nationalism and Culture* (Los Angeles, 1937).

Harold K. Schneider, *Livestock and Equality in East Africa* (Indiana, Bloomington, 1979).

Lysander Spooner, *Let's Abolish Government* (Arno Press, New York, 1972).

Max Weber, *The Theory of Economic and Social Organisation* (Free Press, 1964).

4.
Society Against the State

Pierre Clastres is a French ethnologist specialising in the Indians of the South American tropics. His *Society Against the State** is a structuralist analysis, in the tradition of Claude Levi-Strauss, of the political organisation of these people. At the same time it is a rather ingenious contribution to libertarian (i.e. anarchist) theory.

To appreciate this work, understanding of Levi-Strauss's structuralism is in order. This major theory in contemporary anthropology rests upon Platonist assumptions. There is the external world of appearances and the deep structure of reality – of essences. The task of anthropological investigation is to uncover the latter and so provide an understanding of the universal characteristics of the human mind. Levi-Strauss believes he has discovered one of the fundamental features of that mind: binary opposition. That is, all humans seem to achieve understanding of the world in part at least through classifying phenomena in contrasting pairs. Thus some important dyads are male and female, right and left, culture and nature, donor and receiver. Within the sphere of social relations we discover that reciprocity – the exchange of items of equivalent value between two opposite parties – constitutes a universal underpinning of the social order. In the most archaic societies internal stability and inter-group peace are maintained by the reciprocal exchange of words, women and wealth. So we have a world of givers and receivers, of us and them. As I have suggested, this dualism permeates the human view. Levi-Strauss, professing a debt to Hegel and Marx, claims his theory is also dialectic. Thus a common dyad is the opposition between nature and culture. In the dialectic process nature as thesis yields out of its internal contradictions an antithesis: culture. The opposition or conflict between the two is synthesised or resolved in and through myth. I profess to be no specialist in either Levi-Strauss or philosophy, but I wonder if his binary oppositions are sometimes perhaps not so much dialectic as Kantian antinomies. That is, binary opposites may act not in a dialectic sense but rather as contradictory principles which interact

---

* Pierre Clastres, *Society Against the State*, translated by Robert Hurley (Mole Editions, Urizen Books, New York, 1977).

and conflict without ultimate synthesis, so as to propel society onward
as a moving equilibrium. The reciprocity principle is also treated by
Levi-Strauss much like a Kantian category of mind.

Be that as it may, Pierre Clastres in applying this theoretical
orientation to the political systems of Tropical Indians of South
America argues that a major structural element is the binary
opposition of society against the state. In brief, his case is as follows.

Among these people the chief seems to have no authority to enforce
his will. He cannot legitimately command; that is, he cannot enforce
his orders by a threat of violence. He is, then, not a chief as any
westerner would see it. Real power among these people is vested in
the community as a whole and the chief must always take care lest he
behave in such a manner as to be abandoned by his followers. The
major function of the chief is that of mediator or peace-maker within
the group, but this function should not be confused with the nature
or inner structure of chieftainship. It is this structure which must be
explained, and to do that we must turn to the relationship of the
chiefly role to reciprocity. The chief is involved in an exchange
entailing women, words and wealth. Most of these Indians practice
polygamy. The chief is always the man with the most wives – often
the only polygamist in the group. At the same time the chief is
expected to enthral the group with his oratory – no speech, no chief.
He must sponsor feasts, support the community in hard times, and
always demonstrate his magnanimity and generosity. Through these
mechanisms the chief continually strives to validate and revalidate his
position. But there are not, as one might think, proper reciprocations
to the community for the excess of wives or the position the chief has.
Women are of such 'consummate' value that all the words and all the
gifts provided by the chief are insufficient to qualify the situation as a
reciprocal, that is equal, exchange. As such the chief in his position
defies reciprocity, that basic law of social relations. Such an
asymmetrical relationship is identified with power and that in turn
with nature. In opposition to them stand reciprocity, society and
culture. People in archaic societies realising this conflict and the
contradiction of the fundamental social law see power as enjoying a
privileged position. It is therefore dangerous and in need of restraint.
In fact 'power' should be made 'impotent'. The final synthesis in this
dialectic is paradoxical. The chief's most unreciprocal acquisition of
multiple wives puts him in a condition of perpetual indebtedness to

his people so that he must become their servant. It is this kind of 'leadership' that Orenstein has recently dubbed 'centripetal'.

Clastres's argument is both plausible and logical. Yet reason and logic alone are clearly insufficient grounds for accepting a theory. For the more empirically minded, Clastres's explanation, like other structuralist explanations, seems strangely detached from the solid earth. The use of hard evidence to demonstrate this ingenious theory is lacking. We are given no idea of what the individuals involved may think. But, then, the structuralists argue that these things are superficial appearances, not the world in reality, the deep underlying structure. Structuralism, like Freudianism, Jungianism and, to a lesser extent, Marxism, suffers from the problem of testability. A scientific hypothesis or theory should be so constructed that it is falsifiable. It should be subject to empirical test such that different investigators should be able to analyse the same phenomenon and validate the hypothesis by independently coming to the same conclusions. Strangely enough both Levi-Strauss and Clastres have investigated the chiefly role in South America according to structuralist principles, but have apparently reached different conclusions about it. Quite in contrast to Clastres, Levi-Strauss comes to the conservative conclusion that the chief's gifts of words and wealth for wives is a reciprocal exchange.

Clastres correctly expresses concern about the ethno-centrism inherent in much political anthropology and in cultural evolutionary doctrine, but does it occur to him that perhaps his own structural analysis colours the world with its bias?

In addressing the problem of power Clastres is concerned only with that of the chief. He does not deal with the relations between sexes or the generations. Although there have been countless stateless societies, they, like others, have invariably favoured male dominance, while a patriarchal authoritarianism over the young is perhaps slightly less prevalent.

At least some of the anarchic tropical forest Indians in South America appear to be remnant groups which are the product of decimation and amalgamation of remains of tribes which have faced the onslaught of western society. According to Dole these groups were once more clearly centralised with more powerful chiefs. Dole contends that the strength of the chief's position is tied to lineality – that is, hereditary succession – because it provides a standardised and exclusive channel for the exercise and transmission of authority. With the bringing together of remnant groups, there are several contending claims to chieftainship. The traditional principle of succession is undermined and the authority of any chief is destroyed as a consequence.

Clastres sometimes generalises not only on South American tribal chiefs but for all 'primitive' societies. I suspect, however, that the chief as servant – the 'centripetal' kind of leadership – is represented in only a few such societies. In Australian aboriginal society, the elders constitute a kind of gerontocracy and can compel obedience by threatening to withhold initiation into the esoteric knowledge and rituals held to be essential for the achievement of life's goals. Among Eskimos and throughout New Guinea, influential men are sometimes able to turn the normal anarchy into tyranny. In numerous tribal societies we can clearly see the seeds of the state. Thus the Tiv of central Nigeria possess an anarchistic polity, except within the market place where order is enforced by judges and police. The Ifugao of the Philippines likewise have no state, no law and no government, but important men who act as mediators have the legitimate authority to command on threat of violence the parties to a dispute to engage in the mediation process. Mediators, however, have no authority to enforce a judgement. In a similar vein the leopard-skin 'chief' of the Nuer in the southern Sudan and the rain-maker of the Lugbara of Uganda act as mediators and their only coercive power is the threat to curse those who refuse to abide the decision in a mediation.

Clastres is probably correct if he contends that the state cannot arise directly out of the 'centripetal' type of chiefly role. Nor would it arise out of a situation like that of the Pygmies where there is no formal leadership and the leadership which does exist is assumed with reluctance. But in other cases of what are also anarchic polities, examples of which have been suggested above, we might well see the 'prefiguring' of the state. The development of states is a subtle and insidious process related to the legitimising of an increasing range of unreciprocal or privileged powers of leaders. There are several ways in which this is accomplished. One is to build a following of indebted clients. Another is through control of religious sanctions, as in the Nuer and Lugbara cases above. Hocart has said that the origins of government may be in the role of ritual specialist, a view hinted at by Clastres in considering the role of prophets among the Guarani Indians. Speculation on how the state evolved is largely avoided by Clastres. He does, however, make two comments related to the question which are noteworthy. The shift from hunting-gathering to Neolithic cultivating was not, in his view, such a revolutionary trans- formation because it did not entail that radical an alteration of social structure. The really decisive contrast is between the agricultural tribal community and the nation-state. But here the difference is not in the infrastructure – the technological-economic realm – but in the superstructure – the political organisation. The glaring contrast between the tribal society and the early nation- state is not economic or technological; it is political. The real revolution is the transformation of society into a state with its emphasis upon hierarchical authority and coercive power. As Marx proposed to stand Hegel upon his head, so now Clastres proposes to stand Marx on his head.

On the Marxist theory of the class origin of the state he observes: "If society is organised by oppressors who are able to exploit the oppressed, this is because that ability to impose alienation rests on the use of a certain force, that is, on the thing that constitutes the very substance of the state, 'the monopoly of legitimate physical violence'. That being granted, what necessity would be met by the existence of a state, since its essence – violence – is inherent in the division of society and, in that sense, it is already given in the oppression that one group inflicts on the others? It would be no more than the useless organ of a function that it filled beforehand and elsewhere" (172).

Society Against the State is not purely an essay on political organisation. Clastres addresses the subject of kinship and marriage institutions among tropical forest Indians. He believes they are best described as having exogamous demes. The obligation to marry outside the community operates to establish a network of political alliances and so encourage peaceful relations. Because the distance between houses is so great, and because a woman on marriage moves to her husband's community, this means that the woman is essentially lost to her natal home. She is, then, incorporated into her husband's group. Consequently, according to Clastres, the kin groups do not become unilineal, but rather retain their bilateral or non-linear character.

Clastres also comments on aboriginal South American population estimates, noting that most of them have been entirely too low. Such observations were also made earlier by others, for example Dobyns in 1966.

In a chapter entitled 'The Bow and the Basket' Clastres makes an interesting structural analysis of the social organisation of the hunting-gathering Guayaki. Among them the male is the hunter symbolised by the bow with the masculine space being the hunting grounds. The woman is the collector, symbolised by the basket with her space as the encampment. Hunters are forbidden to eat their own kill and must depend on someone else's. This has the effect of equalising the males. The Guayaki are polyandrous due to a severe shortage of women. Thus, we have a structural analogy: "... Just as a man depends on the hunting of others for his own food, similarly in order to 'consume' his wife, a husband depends on the other husband, whose desires he must respect if co-existence is not to be rendered impossible" (100). Although these techniques operate to ensure the interdependence of the males and the continuation of the society, the men in fact are not satisfied with their lot and often spend their evenings singing songs of protest. Songs "enable them to reject in the domain of language the exchange they are unable to abolish in the domain of goods and women" (102).

While Clastres has here described the Guayaki as polyandrous, he earlier (24) says they are polygynous. One assumes that he means only chiefs are polygynous, a situation which seems to exacerbate an already strained condition.

This book offers many discerning observations on the political process, myth and symbolism. It is suggestive of at least one way in which a people have curbed 'coercive power'. It is a work well worth pondering, although its central thesis should not be accepted uncritically.

Bibliography

Henry F. Dobyns, 'Estimating Aboriginal American Population' in *Current Anthropology* (VII, No. 4, 1966).

Gertrude Dole, 'Anarchy Without Chaos: alternatives to political authority among the Kirikuru' in *Political Anthropology* edited by Mark Swartz, V. Turner and A. Tuden (Aldine Press, 1966).

A.M. Hocart, *Kings and Councillors* (University of Chicago Press, 1970).

Henry Orenstein, 'Asymmetrical Reciprocity: a contribution to the theory of political legitimacy' in *Current Anthropology* (XXI, No. 1, 1980).

5.
Comment on John Zerzan's Critique of Agriculture

John Zerzan's critique of agriculture entails a romanticised notion of hunting-gathering peoples on the one hand and a contrastive highly jaundiced view of the peasant and farm life on the other. Hunter-gatherers do not sit around the fire discussing Plato or the equivalent, or playing games and feasting in a "oneness with nature". As tiny isolated homogeneous communities, they had little intellectual stimulation from outside the narrow confines of their band. They also lacked one of those alienating systems – writing – which is essential to the development and diffusion of highly complex thought. Certainly they produced ideas, some fairly sophisticated, as Paul Radin shows in his *Primitive Man as a Philosopher* (although even here most of the examples are drawn from people who have already succumbed to the evil of agriculture).

Further, the hunting-gathering life may be freer of drudgery than that of a factory worker or nineteenth century peasant. Yet there was 'work', although it might have been in fits and starts: several days of rigorous toil followed by several days of leisure. It is interesting that the examples Zerzan offers are all people of sub-tropical and tropical climates. Life among hunters and gatherers in the sub-arctic and arctic was not so easy and too often was just plain brutal.

Zerzan says production, like work, begins with agriculture, but hunter-gatherers engage in production as well. They produced a great variety of tools, dwellings, clothes, works of art, containers, paints, dyes, medicines, etc., etc. And they even sought to control their external environment. Important in this respect was the controlled burning of different areas so as to manage the types of plants which grew, thus encouraging specific game species. Another less common control was the attempt to divert water resources. It has been suggested that certain divination techniques resulted inadvertently in a kind of

This article was written for the American journal *Fifth Estate* at their request, but was not used. We are publishing it twice: here and in *The Raven 30* on 'New Life to the Land?' which includes contribtions from two 'peasants' who enjoy working on the land. – Freedom Press.

wild game management programme, so that all game in the surrounding vicinity remained at a constant number, one area not becoming depleted while another over-populated. Hunter-gatherers were not nature children. They, too, were 'alienated' and like all humanity lived in that world of culture and symbol so divorced from nature.

Of the longevity of hunter-gatherers Zerzan says "current hunter-gatherers *barring injury and severe infection*, often outlive their civilised contemporaries" (italics added). It is precisely injury and severe infection which took such a toll on these people. Aside from accidents, the mortality of women in childbirth and of infants is important. Zerzan does not mention that hunter-gatherer societies were invariably plagued by sorcery and the frightful domineering power of shamans.

Zerzan is contemptuous of the agricultural life: "the human captivity of being shackled to crops and herds". He joins Marx in believing in the "idiocy of the rural life". Apparently Zerzan is unaware that there are millions of perfectly intelligent human beings who actually enjoy working in the soil and with livestock. They do not view it as drudgery and many would not consider it 'work'. In North America today farmers and ranchers cling tenaciously to their way of life and would dread having to take other employment. There are fewer occupations which allow more personal independence and self-direction. But I cannot delineate here the advantages of an agricultural life, only emphasise that Zerzan's view is dimmed by an urban myopia.

Zerzan blames the curse of work upon agriculture. But clearly pastoralists – those who specialise in herding livestock – are only one example of people who do not regard their activities in maintaining herds as 'work'. Look, for example, at Fulani or East African cattle herders or the horse-cow-sheep herders of Central Asia.

Agriculture, says Zerzan, turned women to beasts of burden and breeders of children. Does he not think women also engaged in these tasks among hunter-gatherers as well? It is pretty clear that the domestication of large draft animals associated with true agriculture relieved women *and men* of acting as beasts of burden.

Zerzan blames domesticated sheep and goats for the denuding of the Circum-Mediterranean forests, but the truth is that the main culprit was humans seeking timber for ship-building and more land to put under the plough.

Zerzan outlines the follies of modern 'agribusiness' and describes the relation of human to domesticated animals as one of domination and breeding for submissiveness. With these views I am generally in accord, yet on the latter subject of domesticated animals he is typically selective in his argument. A species of the intelligence of *Homo sapiens* could hardly have a relationship with cattle, etc., that was not for the most part dominant. After all, a central feature of evolution is adaptation in which inevitably some species compete with others and in so doing one or more become dominant.

One statement of Zerzan's cannot be allowed to pass, particularly since it is an example of his attempt to humanise animals. Zerzan claims that in domesticated animals "courtship is curtailed". The nearest thing to courtship amongst wild relatives of domesticated mammals is the competitive fighting which goes on between rutting males. The sexual relation between male and female is perfunctory – on and off in a matter of a few seconds. There is no 'courtship' here in the wild or in the tame.

One further point on the domestic animal issue. Human-animal relationships are not exclusively those of dominance and submission. There are also those in which humans and animals operate in partnership – or at least they must work together. And the animals even appear to enjoy the tasks, for example dogs in the hunt and in sheep herding or horses cutting and herding cattle, racing and riding in general.

There are presently no satisfactory explanations for the origin of agriculture. Indeed, there may not have been any single cause. For one thing the domestication of plants was independently invented in at least four different places (South West Asia, South East Asia, Central America and West Africa) and there may have been other centres as well. Thus there were different times and different places and so likely different causes. Secondly, the variety of plants and animals were not all domesticated for the same purpose. Domestic fowl were probably domesticated for religious purposes (for use in divination), but there is nothing to suggest such a cause in the domestication of dogs, donkeys or horses.

Zerzan's central thesis is that the origin of agriculture is a part of some massive evolving process of increasing alienation incorporating within it a drive to control and create uniformity. This is very speculative and not a hypothesis one could test. The historical record clearly shows the correlation of agriculture with the state, government, nation, social class and caste, slavery, warfare and militarism, destructive technologies of the urban life. If these are signs of our species alienation and desire for domination, we must ask why are alienation and control apparently so central to humankind. Here I can only throw out a couple of thoughts on this matter. As I have argued, all *Homo sapiens* – hunter-gatherers and agriculturalists alike – are 'alienated' since they are dwellers in the very human world of culture (*cf.*, Ernst Cassirer, *An Essay on Man*). *Homo sapiens* original alienation commenced with the appearance of a brain which was sufficiently intelligent that a sense of self-awareness could arise. The separation of the self from the non-self is the first act of alienation. In our species it appears to be quickly followed by an awareness of our finite existence and probably fifty to a hundred thousand years ago language was invented, initiating that special symbolic world of culture. In short, intelligence in the context of this world would seem to lead to further alienation. As to domination, one universal feature of *Homo sapiens* is the desire for esteem and recognition and the acquisition of influence. The line between this and the 'will to power' is ambiguous indeed.

Certainly modern agriculture needs to be transformed. Mono-cropping, the use of chemical pesticides and fertilisers, feed lots and gasoline engines are only some of the elements of contemporary farming practice which must be challenged and ecologically-sound alternatives introduced. But to suggest that agriculture be abolished is absurd. Zerzan seems to be saying that it should be replaced with hunting-gathering, in which case we'd have to get rid of more than 99% of the world's population, to say nothing of the innumerable good things of life which agriculture and civilisation have brought and which Zerzan, along with the rest of us, takes for granted. Liberation does not come when agriculture disappears. The implication of Zerzan's view is that liberation only comes with death. I would contend that liberation is not absolute. It must be defined within limits circumscribed by the human situation. That human situation currently means, among other things, a world population of nearly six billion. We must find ways to contend with this and at the same time become a more liberated and conserving society. In any case, we cannot contend with such a population without agriculture.

6.
Of People and Chimps

Dudley Young in his *Origins of the Sacred* recapitulates a picture of chimpanzee social behaviour and then proceeds to suggest similar characteristics for early hominids, apparently on the assumption that since there is little genetic difference between humans and chimps we are, therefore, justified in assuming similarities in social features as well. Even more, we are permitted to reconstruct the original behaviour and social life of our earliest ancestors – the Australopithecines, *Homo habilis* and *Homo erectus* – from the chimpanzee data.

Unfortunately Young's is not the only example of this kind of thinking. It seems even implicit in some of the primatological research. I believe it is both erroneous and unjustified. For example, suppose we knew nothing about gorilla social life. If we, therefore, assumed that gorilla social behaviour is consequently very much like that of the chimpanzee we would be wrong. The gorilla social group consists of a single male, several females and immature individuals. The chimp society is multi-male and multi-female in composition. Male coalitions engaging in violent acts against another individual are characteristically chimpanzee; such behaviour is absent among gorillas. Although gorillas do attack and kill their fellows, especially infants, they are on the whole a shy and more gentle lot, sharing a more 'laid-back' society than that of the chimpanzee. The social behaviour of the other great apes – the bonobos, gibbons and orang-utans – is also different from both chimpanzee and gorilla.*

Elsewhere in the animal kingdom similar situations apply. Thus among the closely related species of zebras one species is territorial and others have overlapping ranges. Merely because two species are genetically very closely related does not mean that one can therefore attribute the behavioural characteristics of one to the other.

To ascertain what the earliest human social life was like requires reliance upon the data of human societies. To venture beyond the

---

* On chimpanzee and gorilla social behaviour see, for example, Diane Fossey, 'The Imperial Mountain Gorilla' in *National Geographic* (1981, No. 4, pp. 501-523); *The Great Apes* edited by David Hamburg and E.R. McCown (1979, Benjamin Cummings Publishing Co., Menlo Park, California); *The Mountain Gorilla* by George B. Schaller (1963, University of Chicago).

realm of *Homo sapiens* is perilous to say the least, especially venturing so far afield as into totally different biological families and genera. This means that we should restrict relevant data to the archaeological record and to ethnography. The former supplies us with minimal information. It does, however, show quite clearly that complex and large scale hierarchical and authoritarian organisations appear at best six thousand years ago and that before that time all humans lived in small face-to-face communities with minimal social differentiation. Even as far back as Middle Palaeolithic times (ca 300,000-50,000 B.P.) archaeologists can discern that sharing of food was an important aspect of economic life (Chase, 1989). This is not characteristic of other primates and is suggestive of egalitarian rather than hierarchical social arrangements. The archaeological record further indicates a reduction over time in the size of hominid canines. These teeth are the same size for modern humans as for those who lived fifty thousand years ago, but are smaller than those of the Australopithecines and *Homo habilis* who lived one to three million years ago: "... reduction of canines in hominids suggests less male-male aggression and an increase in overall sociality" (Tanner, 203). Violence was undoubtedly a feature of early human society, but it was much more controlled and less virulent than in ape society. It also lacked the organisation, planning and mass slaughter capability of recent societies.

Ethnography provides us with a much richer array of materials on more contemporary societies. Here the relevant examples would be those which are classed as hunting-gathering or foraging societies, since these are obviously the ones which would be most like the human societies which prevailed throughout the world in ancient times. Having said this it is important to keep a caveat in mind. That is, any more or less contemporary foraging society is still a contemporary society with a history. These people are not our ancestors, nor are they palaeolithic hunters. They are hunters and foragers nevertheless, and we know that all such societies have a number of important features in common. Their subsistence activity places numerous constraints on other aspects of their culture. Hunter-gatherers do not engage in agriculture or animal husbandry. The equestrian nomads of the western American Plains and South American Pampas are not what one could designate as true hunter-gatherers because of their dependence on the horse and consequent development of a horse husbandry. Relying upon wild fauna and flora means that hunter-gatherers, with few exceptions, have only limited resources. The major exception is the west coast American native population which subsisted upon an abundance of fish and marine mammals through which these people accumulated substantial surpluses and elaborated a gift-giving system to enormous proportions. To say that hunter-gatherers have limited resources does not, however, mean that they can only survive on some kind of hand-to-mouth existence. It means rather that there is an adequate supply for a local community, but a capacity to accumulate large supplies of wealth is lacking. Thus differentiation based upon wealth is minimised. At the same time these groups, as small face-to-face entities, lack differentiation in the distribution of power. Why hunter- gatherer societies are 'egalitarian' (at least as far as adult males are concerned) and seem to be more than suspicious of domination are questions which are not to be adequately answered. Boehm has argued that "reverse dominance" occurs in such societies because individuals dislike domination (Boehm, 1993). Others argue for food sharing and pair bonding as having definite survival value or they hold that "egalitarianism ... [is] grounded in inherited tendencies" (Erdal and Whiten, 1994). It is likely that all these factors – and others – are involved (see, for example, Barclay, 1993).

The vast majority of hunting-gathering societies contrast with chimpanzee societies in terms of violence and hierarchical organisation. The ape society is more violent and more given to male dominant hierarchies.

"Simple human societies contrast with both great-ape and middle-range human societies in exhibiting a relative absence of competitive male dominance hierarchies and of systematic violence between closed groups, while being more egalitarian among adult males politically, sexually, and in terms of resource sharing. A U-shaped evolutionary trajectory of selected features of human violence is proposed, with the trough of the curve persisting throughout most of *Homo sapiens* evolution. Simple human societies constitute a major anomaly for models which propose evolutionary similarity between great-apes and pre-state human patterns of violence and suggest a view of human evolution that takes seriously the group selection potential of symbolic transmission" (Knauft, 1991, 391). What Knauft says about the evolution of violence also applies to dominance hierarchies, which are characteristic of chimpanzee society and of more modern human societies, but not of the hunting-gathering societies with which we are familiar.

One might suspect that those who are more prone to derive early human society from the chimpanzee model with its dominance hierarchies are those who may wish to justify similar patterns among humans. They and others who seek to draw on ape examples should beware of such misleading analysis.

Bibliography

Harold B. Barclay's comment on Christopher Boehm's 'Egalitarian Behavior and Reverse Dominance Hierarchy' in *Current Anthropology* (1993, No. 34, p. 255).

Christopher Boehm, 'Egalitarian Behavior and Reverse Dominance Hierarchy' in *Current Anthropology* (1993, No. 34, pp. 227-254).

David Erdal and Andrew Whiten / Christopher Boehm and Bruce Knauft, 'On Human Egalitarianism: an Evolutionary Product of Machiavellian Status Escalation?' in *Current Anthropology* (1994, No. 35, pp. 175-183).

Philip Chase, 'How Different was Middle Palaeolithic Subsistence? A Zooarchaelogical Perspective on the Middle to Upper Palaeolithic Transition' in *The Human Revolution: behavioural and biological perspectives on the origins of modern humans* edited by Paul Mellars and Chris Stringer (1989).

Bruce M. Knauft, 'Violence and Sociality in Human Evolution' in *Current Anthropology* (1991, No. 32, pp. 391-428).

Nancy Makepeace Tanner, *On Becoming Human* (1981, Cambridge University Press).

Dudley Young, *Origins of the Sacred: the ecstasies of love and war* (1992, Harper-Collins, New York).

UTOPIAN AND SOCIAL MOVEMENTS

7.

The Renewal of the Quest for Utopia

Mircea Eliade suggests that much of the exploration and settlement of the western hemisphere is, in part, a search for the earthly paradise or utopia (1966, 260-280). As a new frontier, this hemisphere has long been the desired destination of idealists and dreamers of all sorts. And as a new frontier, it was also particularly amenable to planners, innovators and experimenters. In the United States the 'Yankees' of the north-east, especially, early acquired a reputation as tinkerers and inventors – men with ingenuity. Most concentrated on technology, but there were others who tinkered with plans for a new society. Josiah Warren, for example, tinkered with both. North America was settled by a selective process which drew out adventurers, experimenters and the dissatisfied. It had, then, the proper soil for generating experiments in what have been called utopian communities. Today they are more commonly referred to as intentional communities. This is the more generally appropriate term since members of so many of these communities do not see themselves as achieving the perfect society implied by 'utopian'. Yet all are intentionally seeking alternative forms of social organisation.

The history of Anglo-America over the past two centuries indicates a fluctuating pattern of rise and decline in the interest in such experimentation. Obviously these fluctuations are closely related to socio-economic conditions. While I intend to make a few observations on this particular relationship, I should like to focus first on the extent and intensity of these fluctuations and, secondly, on the major thematic trends in the contemporary movement. Thus in the latter considerations it will be necessary to speak to the issue of presumed 'causes' for the ebb and flow of the utopian movement.

Drawing on several sources (see bibliography), I have compiled a list of 673 communities in the United States and Canada from the earliest settlement to the present. This number includes 175 Hutterian Brethren colonies. However, for the purposes of this paper I intend to concentrate on the 498 non-Hutterian communities. It should be noted further that I have excluded from the list altogether communities which have been initiated by governments, such as those by the United States Farm Security Administration during the late '30s. I cannot pretend that the list is otherwise complete or accurate. Certainly at the rate with which such communities have been established and dissolved, and particularly in the last couple of years, it is impossible to keep track of all such attempts. It is hoped, however, that the data are sufficiently adequate that they can afford a reliable index of significant trends.

In determining whether a given community should be included in this classification I have been guided by the following considerations:

a) That it is treated as an intentional community in the sources.

b) That it is not viewed as a temporary arrangement. Thus I exclude communes which are composed of students or which are summer camps or hostels.

c) That they are not purely centres for the distribution of information about intentional communities (e.g., Carleton Collective Communities, Northfield, Minnesota).

⋆   ⋆   ⋆

While the first half of the nineteenth century is usually viewed as the heyday of utopian experimentation, there can be little doubt that the 1965-69 period has experienced the greatest proliferation of communities. Thus at least 159 were initiated during this time, as against 38 in the comparable period of 1840-44, 23 between 1850-54, 20 between 1880-84 and 19 each in the 1845-49 and 1895-99 periods. In addition, the number initiated between 1965-69 is greater than that for the entire preceding three quarters of a century (1890-1965) during which time 146 such communities were established. It also compares with the 35 which were initiated between 1950 and 1964 just prior to this five-year period.

It is obvious there has been a tremendous resurgence of the intentional community movement, but it may be argued that comparisons of estimates between a contemporary and an early period are misleading, since the reliability of the figures tends to decrease as one moves back in time. Thus one should expect the early period to be under-

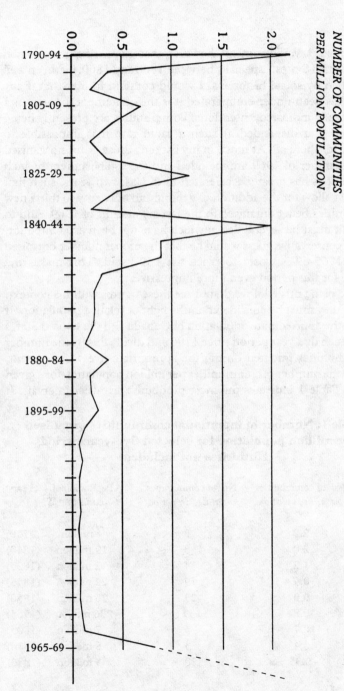

Diagram 1: Number of intentional communities per million population of Canada and the United States at five-year periods

enumerated. I would contend, however, that utopian experimentation in the United States, especially between 1800 and 1860, has been well researched by social historians. I would contend further that if any period has been under-enumerated it is the contemporary one. As I have already indicated, intentional communities are presently being organised and disbanded at such a rapid rate it is impossible to account for them all. At most, in my list only those groups organised by the summer of 1969 are included and the establishment of such communities has greatly accelerated in the last two years, such that one must allow for the addition of a minimum of twenty to thirty new communities being organised in the last six months of 1969. Add to this what must be several dozen which have not been accounted for, and my conservative guess would be that the proper number organised during 1965-69 is closer to twice the 159 listed. This makes the number for this period even more impressive.

We are being misled if we do not see these figures within a context. At least they must be considered in the light of relative population. If we take the approximate population of Canada and the United States during each five-year period since 1790 and divide this by the number of communities initiated during the appropriate five-year segment, we have the number of communities per million population for a given period. Table 1 indicates the most productive five-year intervals. It

Table 1: Number of intentional communities organised per million population for selected five-year periods (Hutterites not included)

Years	No. of communities per 1m population	No. of communities organised in period	Population of Canada & US	(Years)
1790-94	2.2	9	4 million	(1790)
1840-44	2.0	38	19 million	(1840)
1825-29	1.2	14	12 million	(1825)
1845-49	0.9	19	22 million	(1845)
1850-54	0.9	23	26 million	(1850)
1965-69	0.8	159	206 million	(1965)
1805-09	0.7	5	7 million	(1805)
1810-14	0.4	3	8 million	(1810)
1880-84	0.35	20	55 million	(1880)

indicates that the greatest proliferation in relation to population size was between 1790 and 1794 when the Shaker communal movement was begun. This is followed by 1840-44, a period of Fourierist florescence, and 1825-29 when most Owenite communities were organised. The present period is about on a par with those of 1845-49, 1850-54 and 1805-09 and if, as was suggested above, one even doubles the number of communities for 1965-69 the number per million population (1.6) has not reached the degree of the 1790-94 or 1840-44 periods. In other words, when looking at the number of communities alone the contemporary period appears fantastically out of proportion to any other. When placed in the context of population, the number suggests that the resurgence of the movement is closely approximate to that of the first half of the nineteenth century, although it is not as intensive as two five-year periods within that time: 1790-94 and 1840-44. If present rates continue, and there is every reason to believe they are not about to abate, the prospect for 1970-74 is that the movement will surpass any past period.

Table 2 indicates the types of community experiment as they are distributed over time. Several of the categories are imprecise and impressionistic. Thus a great number of communities, among them many so-called hippie communes, are 'anarchistic' but are not included in that category primarily because their roots do not come out of the mainstream of the anarchist movement *per se*. Similarly, many communities are 'pacifist' but are classed elsewhere because that view does not appear to be as important an identifying tag as some other. Accepting the limitations of this crude classification, we may note the following.

The two periods 1790-1809 and 1810-1829 produced 39 community endeavours of which 12 were along lines suggested by Robert Owen and 17 were Shaker colonies. During the peak period, 1830-1849, almost half the experiments (32 out of 67) were Fourierist; 20 were religious of different sorts, including Mormon, Oneida and the first Amana community. From 1850-69 there is a general decline, but the number and proportion of religious experiments increases. Of 47 communities, 29 are religious, including seven Mormon and seven Amana. While 32 Fourierist experiments were initiated between 1841 and 1849, between 1850 and 1870 only three such communities were established. Following the Civil War, the movement declined and its character changed. Between 1870 and 1909, 79 communities were

Table 2: Types of intentional communities in United States and Canada 1790-1969

Type	Total	Pre 1790	1790-1809	1810-1829	1830-1849	1850-1869	1870-1889	1890-1909	1910-1929	1930-1949	1950-1969
SECULAR	245	0	1	12	47	17	17	27	19	11	94
Owenite	14			12	2						
Fourierist	35				32	3					
Anarchist	16				4	1	1	2	1	1	6
Icaria	6				2	3	1				
Alcander Longley	7					2	5				
Socialist cooperatives	31						4	20	5	2	
Little Landers	5							1	4		
Single tax	11							4	6	1	
Urban communes	47									1	46
Group marriage, etc.	8										8
Walden Two	4										4
Non-religious pacifist	2										2
Other	59		1		7	8	6		3	6	28
RELIGIOUS	207	13	16	10	20	29	21	14	9	21	54
Shaker	19	2	13	4							
Moravian	6	4				2					
Dorrelite	2		2								
Rappite	3		1	2							
Rappite splinter	3				3						
Jewish	22				1		16	2	1	2	
Mormon	15				5	7	1			1	1
Oneida	5				3	2					
Roman Catholic	7				1	1				4	1
Amana	8				1	7					
Thos. Lake Harris	3					3					
Dukhobor	4							1	1	2	
Quaker	5									2	3
Christian Pacifist	9									7	2
Esoteric	25									1	24
Conservative Christian	14										14
Other	57	7		4	6	7	4	11	7	2	9
UNCLASSIFIED	46										46
HUTTERIAN BRETHREN	175							17	27	55	76
	673	13	17	22	67	46	38	41	55	87	270

17

established, 44 non-religious and 35 religious. Of the non-religious more than half (24) were what may be classed as socialist cooperative communities and of the 35 religious colonies 18 were Jewish, reflecting the combined influence of socialist and Zionist doctrine on that segment of the population. The fifty-year period from 1910-49 produced only 60 communities of a variety of kinds. Notable among these were still more socialist cooperatives, the single tax (Henry Georgist) common land settlements, and several Christian pacifist communities largely organised by conscientious objectors in response to World War Two. The four Roman Catholic communities were established at different times by adherents to Peter Maurin's Catholic Worker movement.

As I have already suggested, the great resurgence of the utopian movement since 1950 has primarily been concentrated in the period since 1965. Of at least 194 communities (27 in Canada) 94 are secular and 54 are religious; for 46 others data is insufficient to indicate their ideological base. Among the religious experiments there has been a florescence of esoteric communities in which I have included self-styled 'hip communes' as well as flying saucer and Buddhist groups. Thirteen others are essentially classifiable as conservative Biblicist Christian, including six which derive from the Hutterites. Notable among the secular groups is the proliferation of urban communes and, also, those primarily dedicated to radical sexual reforms such as free love or group marriage. Interestingly enough, the work of B.F. Skinner has proved the inspiration for a small movement (Walden Two) which has resulted, thus far, in at least four communities, and I have heard recently of an Edmonton group which was planning a Walden Two in the Peace River area.

*   *   *

For the first half of the nineteenth century utopian experimentation is in large part a positive response to the challenge of the frontier and a negative response to the changing character of American society, at least in the eastern sector. A considerable segment of the utopian movement of this time might properly be considered as part of the agrarian populist movement reacting to the shift from a rural, agrarian America to an industrial urban society operated no longer by handicraft enterprises but by steam-powered engines and the factory system. Indeed, the persistent search for the arcadian commune stands as a protest against the increasing impersonality and alienation provoked by the urban capitalist factory system and at the same time it was an impetus to the development of the middle western parts of the United States. Further, the movement in North America was closely tied to theoretical developments in Europe. Theoretical models spun in Europe were, so to speak, worn in North America.*

In large part the decline of the utopian movement around 1860 can be attributed to the disruptive effects of the Civil War, the obvious failure, especially, of the secular communities and the related search, again inspired in large part by European radicals, for new techniques for the expression of discontent: the development of radical political parties, farmer and labour organisations. It is interesting to note that radical and populist electoral activity in the United States is most evident during the period from the 1870s to the early 1950s. This is also the period for the lowest communal activity. From 1800 to the Civil War and the period since 1960 are the peaks of utopian experimentation in that country, as well as periods of minimal radical electoral activity. Certainly during the latter period, since 1960, it can readily be argued that major portions of the populist-radical forces in America have become disillusioned with trying to achieve the revolution through the ballot box and have tended to revert to the early nineteenth century technique of practical implementation of the revolution.

An increasing sense of desperation, helplessness and frustration, especially in youth circles, at existing institutions has created a new radicalism.** The new radical notes that despite how he may cast his vote, the wars get bigger and more brutal, the industrial-military complex more gigantic, centralisation and bureaucratisation more the order of the day and the 'system' more oppressive. What, then, can one do? One can try to save himself, and any others who will heed the message, by the initiation of communes which seek to re-establish the human values inherent in primary relations, meaningful work and respect for individuality.

---

* This is not to overlook the fact that large numbers of intentional communities have also been organised in Europe.

** Boredom and affluence are other factors which a more careful examination might reveal as important motivating forces, especially with regard to some of the more bizarre manifestations in the movement.

Thus, among the main messages of the contemporary community movement is propaganda by example. Another is the emphasis upon personal transformation as well as the transformation of the social order. Overall, there is a revulsion against structure, planned societies and authoritarian systems and an affirmation of freedom and individuality, which is in sharp contrast to much of the earlier utopian experimentation. 'Do your own thing' is stressed, but as it is a reaction to established traditional authorities it too tends to set up its own hidebound traditional authority. Thus in the hippie commune appears the new conformity to long hair and bare feet.

On the one hand the 'do your own thing' philosophy stresses the positive goal of freedom and, on the other, it can encourage or even be a disguise for irresponsibility and a selfish egotistic lack of concern for others. One expression of this is exemplified by those hippie commune members who survive not only because they minimise their personal needs, but because of the financial support they expect and accept from their establishment-oriented middle-class parents. (Possibly it should be borne in mind that certain monastic orders have somewhat similar arrangements.)

It is, of course, true that some recent experimentation has a definitely authoritarian flavour, as in the Christian conservative colonies. One might expect that in a time of stress there would be a tendency for individuals to follow one of two diametrically opposed paths: the libertarian or the authoritarian. (This dichotomy makes more sense today in many political discussions than does the distinction between radical and conservative.) Obviously, the prevalent trend today is in the libertarian direction.

The contemporary anarchistic trend in utopian experimentation is nothing new. What is new is that is has become of major importance in the movement. Similarly, a partiality to esoteric mystical doctrine and to radical experimentation in sexual relations is by no means new to the movement. In the nineteenth century Swedenborgianism, Transcendentalism, Spiritualism, Theosophy and Mormonism were the esoteric doctrines of the day and were common to many intentional communities. These doctrines have, of course, become respectable with the passage of time. Today we have Zen, flying saucer cults, various branches of Hinduism and the like. In the nineteenth century there was the radical sexual experimentation of the Shakers, the Mormons and Oneida communities. Today, there are the group marriage communes.

The drug cult does signify a new trend for which there appears to be no nineteenth century parallel in the utopian movement, except in the stress on mysticism. But, then, the drug cult in other contexts is as old as the hills.

Another new trend in the intentional community movement is the urban commune, some of which bear similarities presumably to the early Christian community or certain types of medieval guild organisation with the common house, common table, pooling of resources while each plies his trade working for wages in the community. Somewhat similar is the rural community which does not depend on agriculture but produces handicrafts or provides services such as schools or rehabilitation homes. The following table (Table 3) indicates the results for 121 communities for which there is adequate information, showing not only the urban emphasis but also the non-agricultural character of such communities.

The trend away from agricultural communities follows the national patterns in Canada and the United States of the decline of agriculture and, also, is a practical turn in light of the overwhelming urban, non-agricultural backgrounds of individuals joining the movement. It also contrasts with the rural agricultural orientation of most previous utopian experimentation. It should be noted that the proliferation of

Table 3: Contemporary intentional communities as rural/urban and agricultural/non-agricultural enterprises (Hutterites excluded)

	Agricultural	*Non-agricultural*	*Total*
Religious Communities			
Rural	10	11	21
Urban	0	15	15
	10	26	36
Secular Communities			
Rural	17	12	29
Urban	0	56	56
	17	68	85
TOTAL	*27*	*94*	*121*

rural intentional communities may, in many areas, have the effect of revitalising a declining countryside.

By way of conclusion, I wish to recapitulate the following points:

1) There has been an enormous increase in community experimentation in the past half decade, but when taking population into consideration it is likely that the extent of such experimentation did not reach certain of the comparable peak periods of the earlier heyday of the movement. We are now on the ascendant side of what is the greatest cresting in the history of the movement.

2) The increase in such groups is attributable to causes similar to, yet different from, those which provoked the earlier nineteenth century florescence. The sources of the modern resurgence are to be found in the desperation and feeling of helplessness and frustration within the existing structures.

3) When radical-populist electoral activity in the United States has been strong, utopian experimentation has been weak, and when the latter is strong the activity at the ballot box is weak. This would suggest that these techniques for the expression of popular discontent are not always mutually compatible. In other words, the communal movement tends to be more 'escapist'.

4) The major thematic trends in the contemporary intentional community movement are for the most part by no means new. The non-agricultural and urban character of so many new communes and the introduction of the drug cult into the movement can be considered innovative. While anarchistic ideology has always been a somewhat minor undercurrent, it has today become a major stream.

Finally, in the disillusionment by youth and others of us with the world as it is, the reaction of helplessness and frustration often provokes irrational violent and frantic outbursts – burnings, destruction of physical symbols of the establishment and assaults upon its defenders. The intentional community movement, which derives from the same sources of discontent, takes a constructive direction, stressing the focusing of individual initiative on creating something new within the shell of the old. With all its faults and shortcomings – and they are certainly many – the renewed quest for the community of the good life puts a refreshing emphasis within the radical-populist movement upon creative constructivity, individual initiative, responsibility and freedom – a welcomed contrast to the violence and Marxist totalitarianism of others.

Bibliography

Ralph Albertson, 'A Survey of Mutualist Communities in America' in *Journal of History and Politics* (XXXIV, 1936, pp. 375-444).

Edward A. Andrews, *The People Called Shakers* (New York, 1963).

Harold Barclay, 'Josiah Warren: The Incompleat Anarchist' in *Anarchy* (VIII, 1968, pp. 90-96).

Arthur Bestor, *Backwoods Utopias: The Sectarian and Owenite Phases of Communitarian Socialism in America 1663-1829* (Philadelphia, 1950).

Fred A. Bushee, 'Communistic Societies in the United States' in *Political Science Quarterly* (XX, 1905, pp. 625-664).

Directory of Social Change, *Modern Utopian* (Medford, Massachusetts, 1967).

Directory of Social Change, *Modern Utopian* (Berkeley, California, 1969).

Mircea Eliade, 'Paradise and Utopia: Mythical Geography and Eschatology' in *Utopias and Utopian Thought* edited by Frank Manuel (Boston, 1965).

William A. Hind, *American Communities* (Chicago, 1902).

Robert V. Hine, *California's Utopian Colonies* (Yale, New Haven, 1966).

Henrik Infield, *Cooperative Group Living* (New York, 1950).

W. McKinley, 'A Guide to Communistic Communities of Ohio' in *Ohio State Archaeological and Historical Quarterly* (XLVI, 1937, pp. 1-15).

Charles Nordhoff, *The Communistic Societies of the United States* (New York, 1875).

John H. Noyes, *History of American Socialisms* (New York, 1961).

Everett Webber, *Escape to Utopia* (New York, 1959).

Julie E. Williams, 'An Analytical Tabulation of the North American Utopian Communities by Type, Longevity and Location', MA Thesis, University of South Dakota, 1939.

8.
Argenta, British Columbia: An Experiment in Community

One of the most common features about intentional experiments in community living is their short lifespan. I propose in this paper to describe one kind of community experiment in Argenta, British Columbia, which has managed to carry on for twenty years, a rather lengthy existence comparatively speaking. From the description I would like to draw certain propositions which may help to explain why Argenta has survived.

Background

Argenta is a dispersed rural neighbourhood on the north-eastern edge of Lake Kootenay, British Columbia. In this mountainous and rather marginal and sparsely populated region, lumbering is the chief industry, while limited amounts of tourism, cattle ranching and mixed farming are important.

In 1952 two Quaker families from California settled in Argenta, to be followed in the ensuing two years by four other families. These new settlers chose Argenta as a rural region with inexpensive land where they might experiment in some kind of more communal life and escape the hyper-urbanisation of California and all it signified to them. Since 1954 there has been a trickle of settlers with corresponding ideas who have moved into the vicinity, so that by 1969 the community had a permanent population of about 80 with a total of 22 families. Of these, six families resided here for non-ideological reasons and for the most part represented individuals who settled in the neighbourhood before 1950. Sixteen families were residents of Argenta because of ideological commitment, and it is these that therefore comprise the Argenta ideological community, the topic of this paper.

Initially Argentans experimented with different kinds of cooperative economic enterprises, even at one time establishing a cooperative association to engage in farming, logging and handicrafts. This experiment failed, in part because much of the proposed programme, especially the logging scheme, proved impractical for them but also it was found they 'couldn't get along' in such an arrangement.

Service occupations today provide the main source of income. The largest single number of people are employed by the Friends' School while others work for the forestry service or are teachers in nearby schools. Although most are homesteaders, none are totally or even primarily dependent on the land for a livelihood.

Ideology

No precise ideology binds Argentans together. Less than half are actually Quakers and, since they are the only organised group in the community and were early entrenched within it, they are also the most influential. In addition, like Quakers elsewhere, their influence tends to be greater than their numbers would indicate.

Friends' emphasis on the individual experience of the inner light in the context of an undirected meeting of silent worship has meant a de-emphasis upon form, structure and hierarchy. Since there is that of God in every man, every individual is worthy of respect and love. Thus have Friends traditionally placed stress upon individual liberty, tolerance for differences and a refusal to employ violence under any circumstances.

The 'quietistic' aspect of Quakerism has not resulted in Friends seeking annihilation of self or deliverance from the world. Rather silent meditation to receive the inner light is viewed as a device to better prepare the individual for working in the world to improve it. Both the passive and the active aspects are conceived as forms of worship. However, within the dimension of the action-orientation a polar tension has developed between the more materialistic business-man's shrewdness and the more idealistic concept of social service. Thus, Quakerism has produced such divergent phenomena as Richard Nixon on the one hand and the Friends' Service Committee on the other.

Quakers have, then, not been 'escapists' and thus have not been prominent in the organisation of utopian communities. Argenta is one of the few Quaker inspired examples along such lines. Yet even here Friends engage most noticeably in community services: they organised and maintained a Friends' School, a high school level institution which draws students from both Canada and the United States. They have been most active in the Argenta community centre providing adult education classes and a number of other services.

If Argenta is not specifically a Quaker community at least the flavour of Quakerism goes beyond the bounds of the Friends themselves. Thus a major ideological theme shared in Argenta stresses individuality and freedom and rejects regimentation and bureaucratisation. It is summed up by the words 'Do Thy Thing' which are carved on the rough walls of a building at Argenta Friends' School. For many, however, there are limits to what one may do. As is noted below, disagreement exists over use of drugs and about sexual behaviour. What is characteristic of Argenta compared to a more standard Canadian rural community is that the limits of toleration are far broader.

Argenta as a community
Argenta is today a loosely-knit social entity in which the sense of community arises out of the fact that the residents settled the vicinity for similar ideological reasons. The rather broad commonly held orientation sketched above lends a continuing sense of community which is reinforced by the mutual interest a majority of the residents have in one way or another in the Friends' School, in the organisation and maintenance of a community centre and in general community concerns which have arisen as a result of their living as neighbours to one another. Thus an attempt by the government and lumber interests to construct a logging road through the area led to a consolidated protest action by members of the community. In a fashion reminiscent of a segmentary lineage structure, this presumably loose collection of homesteaders when threatened by an outside force became a solitary community unit marshalling itself against the external threat.

No formal community organisation exists. Any necessary group actions, as in the above case, are initiated on an *ad hoc* basis. Friends' meetings and the Friends' School are administered by the Friends in their meeting for business, which operates according to the 'sense of the meeting' – a consensual technique which rests on the principle of unanimous consent before action can be taken and so shows greater concern for minority rights than does democratic procedure. It is likewise conducive to extended discussion. Indeed, 'talk' has been alleged to be a major activity in Argenta as a whole (Gray, 1961). With such a large proportion of residents coming from a Friends milieu it might be expected that group decision would entail a lengthy process, but even among the non-Friends 'talk' has been important. One informant referred to Argenta as 'Argenda', intimating that the community was probably too often hampered by the amount of discussion which went on.

Personal behaviour of individuals has led to some internal disagreement within Argenta. The great majority have opposed the use of drugs and marijuana, yet there are summer transient visitors and students at the Friends' School who use them. Within the school, students have been expelled for persisting in their use, but no internal mechanisms exist to control others outside the Quaker group. The practice of communal nude bathing among some has caused other Argentans to raise their eyebrows, and there is a distinct difference of opinion about the extent to which pre-marital sexual relations among adolescents should be tolerated and about the related issue of the need for chaperoning adolescent parties which are sometimes held at the community centre. Certainly these issues are not unique to Argenta, nor is the fact that they have remained unresolved issues for which no consensus exists. What tends to be unique is, as was stated earlier, that Argentans are more permissive of deviance.

One informant described the difference of opinion in Argenta as opposition between one group which was interested in experimentation and innovation and the other, the Friends, who were conservative and rigid. In any case, those associated with the Friends do stand for a more restrained position. They disapprove of nudist practices, although they are not about to suggest to others that they cannot or should not indulge in them. They are also opposed to unchaperoned parties, illicit sexual relations and strongly opposed to the use of drugs. Their education views, as well, express greater adherence to tradition – all recognise the need for structure, but there is among them some difference, the principal of the Friends' School being more 'liberal' in his views of education than, for example, another Friend who happens to teach in the public school and believed Argenta Friends' School is not structured enough. A more radical or 'experimental' group holds contrasting opinions, in that while its supporters may not use drugs themselves or engage in illicit sexual relations, they do not oppose these practices. They tend to have more radical views about education as well. Although these two contrasting groups may be identified in Argenta, a very considerable number of residents would not be found associated with either of them.

One should not assume from the foregoing discussion that Argenta Friends are conservative; they are so only in relation to certain individuals in Argenta. And there are those in the North Kootenay vicinity who readily view the Friends as hippies and revolutionaries. In terms of the total population of the area, the Friends obviously represent a 'left' of the middle group between the 'non-ideological' residents on the one hand and those more sympathetic to 'hippie' manners on the other.

Other so-called 'intentional' or 'utopian' experiments in community have more frequently been organised around a very specific ideology and a more rigid pattern of social organisation which gives the community distinctness and definite form. Argenta points to an alternative technique for community: the loose neighbourhood of roughly ideologically congenial families who pursue cooperative effort where this appears by consensus to be fruitful and go about their own affairs otherwise. Compared to other experiments in community, Argenta has survived a considerable length of time and all prospects are that as it now exists it will continue to persist. In addition there has been a notable stability in residence. Six families have resided in Argenta for over ten years and another four for from five to ten years. The greatest amount of turnover results from employment of teachers at the Friends' School, some of whom accept positions without always intending to make Argenta their life career.

It is, however, interesting to note that several families have now raised their children to adulthood and the overwhelming majority of these offspring have moved elsewhere, back into the mainstream of Canadian life. Few have chosen to remain in Argenta or seek a life in another similar community. Argenta's children have been taught and are taught to make their own decisions about careers; there is no negative sanction against leaving the community. Further, they are taught a full awareness of the world and, while Argentans prefer to remain aloof from the world in certain ways, in others they are very much a part of it and involved with it. Argenta, of course, lacks many facilities and means for a livelihood for these children and the invitation to explore the world induces many of them to acquire interests which can in no way be satisfied in Argenta. Finally, it is necessary to bear in mind that Argenta children have been reared in a cultural context quite different from the usual urban American middle-class of most of their parents, so that their personal problems are not always those of their parents. These factors and combinations of them may suggest why it is that Argenta children are not retained in the community.

The *Maclean's* articles (1961, 1968) have provoked inquiries about Argenta and to these Argentans are quick to indicate that theirs is not an intentional community and equally quick to discourage new converts, although in the past year – aside from those employed by the Friends' School – two new families have settled in Argenta. Argenta has become rather widely known. Especially during the summer months, transient 'hippies' hitch-hike into the community and rent an old shack or live for a while with a member of the community who happens to be acquainted with many people in Vancouver. When the cold of winter sets in, these people rapidly evaporate. They are a source of conflict in the community in that it is largely through this group that drugs enter Argenta. Secondly, several of the non-ideological residents in Argenta view their intrusion as further substantiation of their belief that the Quakers and their associates are part-and-parcel of a decadent dope-ridden, long-haired, bare-footed way of life which has spelled the doom of Argenta.

Why has Argenta survived?

There are several reasons that account for Argenta's survival. I shall mention four of them. First, Argentans have not sought in their experimentation to deviate radically from standard social practices. Too many communities have collapsed in large part because they have tampered too radically with the social order of which they are a part. This has invariably led to extremely difficult relations with outsiders to the point of downright oppression and interference by public authorities. More important is the fact that radical innovation, especially with the family and marital systems, inevitably invites participants who are struggling with their own emotional problems. Further, participation in radical sexual experimentation invariably provokes its own conflicts, both inter- and intra-personal, since there is too much of a residue of traditional conceptions of morality, property, etc., to afford peace of mind to the individual in a very different social context.

Secondly, part of the fact that Argentans have not deviated radically from their own past cultural traditions has been the continued, indeed greater, emphasis on privacy and individual freedom. One of the major pitfalls of much utopian experimentation has been the attempt to impose, in what amounts to a revolutionary transformation, an authoritarian, communal and very public social order upon a people whose values are individualistic and libertarian. One can in community experimentation so bind the members together with a multitude of mutual obligations and commitments that they are motivated to make the system work, if only because of the extent of their personal investment in it. On the other hand, such arrangements which seem to demand continual intense social interaction, as well as the facing of difficult issues of allocation of power and decision-making and the assumption of responsibility at every turn, are fraught with potentially devastating conflict situations. In Argenta each family remains an autonomous unit in some degree of isolation from others. Cooperation between them is on a voluntary basis and overall community regulation is minimal. The Quakerly values of tolerance and understanding are combined with the old Western American norm of minding one's own business. Thus open conflicts potentially destructive of the community are avoided. Conflict and hostility itself may not be dissipated, but the situations which might generate an explosion are avoided or at least held to a minimum.

Thirdly, Argentans have been committed neither to a rigid and doctrinaire programme nor to salvation by a single panacea. They have displayed a sufficient degree of flexibility, a diversity of interest and pragmatism to allow them to pursue other alternatives when one experiment fails. Thus the cooperative enterprise mentioned above was never so much a foundation stone of the community that when it failed the community went down with it. Rather, Argentans adjusted their life pattern to a slightly different tune.

Fourthly, the pragmatic or practical orientation reveals itself in still another way. That is, levels of expectation have not been so high as to provoke intense disappointment in the face of trouble. No one who has stayed on at Argenta, in other words, has expected utopia or the millennium. A shed at the Friends' School bears the label 'Utopia'. One of the teachers at the school, and a long-time Argenta resident, remarked that "That is the only place you'll find it in Argenta. It certainly doesn't exist anywhere else."

Community experimentation sometimes faces severe pitfalls because the participants are in a very real sense impractical dreamers, not only in their expectation but also in their preparation for community life. Thus they come to the community with exquisite visions which are soon demolished, more often than not traumatically. They come to a community ignorant of the most basic knowledge of making a living. For example, there are those who have been reared and lived their entire lives in large metropolitan cities, who have no first-hand knowledge of rural life or agriculture and yet intend to live, usually on highly marginal land, as some kind of subsistence farmers. Argentans have, on the other hand, managed to apply themselves to those endeavours which are congenial to them, while at the same time adapting to the surrounding environment and remaining economically solvent.

In sum, Argenta has survived because it has not tried too much to defy established standards or to alter past cultural values of the community members. One could even say that the main reason for the removal to Argenta was, in the narrow sense of the term, a conservative one: the aim of preserving many traditional values that individuals felt were being threatened in urban California. In addition, Argentans have been flexible, eclectic and practical, embracing a loosely structured social system. These elements largely reflect the dominant Quaker ideology.

Obviously there are a multitude of paths to community survival, but I suspect they all will show, like Argenta, strong indications of pragmatism, flexibility and not too radical a break with the past cultural traditions to community members. The danger to Argenta's future is that its very looseness, its pragmatism and lack of very distinct social boundaries may readily contribute to its gradual absorption into the mainstream 'great society'.

Bibliography

Argenta Friends' School *Newsletter* (Argenta, British Colombia)

Argenta Friends' School *Student Handbook* (no date).

Howard Brinton, *The Pendle Hill Idea* (Pendle Hill Pamphlet #55, Pendle Hill Publications, Wallingford, Pa., 1950).

John Gray, 'How Seven Families *Really* Got Away From It All' in *Maclean's* (7th October 1961).

'Green Power' in *Maclean's* (May 1968).

Norman J. Whitney, *Experiments in Community* (Pendle Hill Pamphlet #149, Pendle Hill Publications, Wallingford, Pa., 1966).

9.
Populism

Populism is a word which has been applied to an extremely wide range of social phenomena and often employed with little precision. In this collection of essays* several scholars from various social sciences and different countries (although a majority are British) seek to explicate the term. The first part of the book includes essays on populist manifestations in North America (Richard Hofstadter), Latin America (Alistair Hennessy), Russia (Andrzej Walicki), Eastern Europe (Ghita Ionescu) and Africa (John Saul). Part two considers 'Populism as an Ideology' (Donald MacRae), 'A Syndrome, Not a Doctrine' (Peter Wiles), 'The Social Roots' (Angus Stewart), 'Populism as a Political Movement' (Kenneth Minogue) and a final summary article by Peter Worsley, 'The Concept of Populism'.

I do not propose to present an essay-by-essay run-down but, rather, wish to cover some of the major attributes of populism which arise out of the book as a whole. I shall describe the most general characteristics of populism which, following Worsley, we may call its 'genus' traits, and then consider the species within the genus.

Worsley modifies an earlier definition by Edward Shils to offer the broadest conceptualisation of populism. He calls it an 'emphasis' on 'popular participation'. By using participation, Worsley rightly indicates that populism can be either 'democratic' or 'non-democratic'. Worsley and other authors in this book clarify what lies behind this idea of popular participation. On the positive side is the belief in the "virtues of the uncorruptible, simple, common folk" while on the negative is a distrust for the 'smart', the 'aristocratic', the 'over- educated', etc. In Hofstadter's words there is the belief in "an essentially innocent folk, victimised by economic catastrophes for which it shared no responsibility", the division "between 'the people' who worked for a living and the vested interests who did not". The underlying theme, then, is one of the good small guys versus the bad big guys who are invariably outsiders. Populism to Donald MacRae is romantic primitivism, not of the tribe but of the agrarian *Gemeinschaft* and its

* *Populism: Its Meanings and National Characteristics*, edited by Ghita Ionescu and Ernest Gellner (Weidenfeld & Nicolson, London, 1969).

most typical feature "in a way is its theory of personality". For
MacRae, populism combines "rebellion against the alienated human
condition, the idea that integral personality was maimed by the social
division of labour, a belief in the sacredness of the soil and those who
tilled it, a faith in belonging to a local, fixed, virtuous and consensual
community, and a belief that this virtue could only perish by usurpation,
conspiracy and the working of active, alien, urban vice". MacRae, it
seems to me, here pins down crucial characteristics of any populism
except that the emphasis on the sacred soil and those who till it is
more often to be identified with a particular species of populism:
agrarian populism. Angus Stewart notes the Janus-headed quality of
populism. It looks back to tradition and forward to modernisation
and believes it can control the latter process and bring a synthesis of
the two – traditionalism and modernism. Thus while Marxism preaches
the opposition between capitalism and proletariat and the ultimate
synthesis in socialism, populists argue the opposition of traditionalism
and modernism, with populism as its synthesis. Stewart quotes Shils'
observation that populism is "a phenomenon of the tension between
metropolis and province" and goes on to argue "that a necessary
condition for the emergence of populism ... has been contact with
forces and ideas associated with higher levels of development than
those to be found in the society producing the response". Populism
becomes a response to the 'crisis of development'. In this respect it is
appropriate to mention John Saul's reference to Barrington Moore's
suggestion that radicalism's social basis may not be so much on a new
rising social class as "the dying wail of a class". Populism has been
especially important among farmers, peasants and other segments of
the population who are threatened by the modern world. Populism is
a reaction, not only to alienation of the individual but to a threat to
group existence, and is thus in a very real sense a revitalisation
movement, specific manifestations of which may be classed, following
Anthony Wallace, as Revivalistic, Utopian, Expropriative or Assimilative
(*Religion: An Anthropological View*, Random House, 1966).

The genus populism, it seems to me, has three clearly defined
species, defined primarily on the basis of the interest groups involved:

1) Agrarian Populism
   Subspecies: Farmer
   Subspecies: Peasant

2) Third World Populism

3) Urban Bourgeois Populism

Agrarian Populism, more than other populisms, directs its appeal to a specific segment of the population: the cultivators. Populism is generally viewed as a political ideology which cuts across classes, avoids class war and appeals to all the 'hinterland' folks. But in agrarianism there is a stress on a single occupational group. However, it can be argued that this is not a class appeal so much as a regional appeal: most of those in the hinterland are cultivators and the remainder are primarily dependent upon them and have agrarian values. Agrarian populism stresses what MacRae calls the "sturdy yeoman ideal", the "sacred farm" and the "good times of the peasant community". There are two distinct subspecies. Farmer populism of the United States, Canada, Australia, Scandinavia and France represents the independent cultivator entrepreneur whose interest is in easy credit and good markets, leading to programmes which emphasise money reform and often a conspiracy theory which can reach its extreme in the concept of the International Conspiracy of Jewish Financiers. The peasant populism of Eastern Europe represented the small, more subsistence oriented cultivators, most of whom were landless tenants and, thus, while it too was concerned about credit and markets, its stress and interest was in land reform and the breaking up of large estates.

A second species of populism is Third World Populism. It appeals across all classes and segments to the whole 'hinterland' nation. It is more clearly allied with nationalism and, as Worsley states, would be nationalism were it not for its heavy emphasis upon a social programme. Third World Populism differs, in part, from agrarian populism in its emphasis on communalism. It supports a 'mixed economy' tending towards a kind of pragmatic socialism. It sees the Party State as the vehicle of development and is explicitly identified with the need for industrialisation. Third World Populism most often considers the Party as the expression of a *gemeinschaftlich*, peasant style 'consensualism'. Some Third World populisms seem less Janus- headed than others, more pragmatic and oriented to modernisation, thus, for example, Bourguiba's Tunisia.

A third species, urban bourgeois populism, has primarily non-agrarian associations. It makes no class or occupational appeal but attracts more alienated groups of the modern industrial urban culture such as the new migrants to the city, the small shopkeepers or the elderly. Such organisations as Coughlin's National Union for Social Justice or the Townsend Movement in the United States, Social Credit in British Columbia, Poujadism in France or Peronism in Argentina are of this kind.

An important issue to which this book could have devoted more space is the relation of fascism to populism. In an excellent book, *The Ideology of Fascism* (Free Press, 1967), A. James Gregor argues, in part, that fascism can be seen as a reaction by marginal or economically depressed European states – post World War One Italy, Spain and Germany – and thus may be viewed in the populistic context of the hinterland-metropolis model. Gregor delineates the several attributes of fascism and so further indicates the degree to which fascism shares a common outlook with populism: opposition to and avoidance of a class orientation, emphasis on national or regional solidarity, its stress on the moral superiority of Das Volk, and corresponding suspicion of intelligentsia, foreigners, financiers and the like, usually leading to a conspiracy theory of history, the appeal to consensus and the emphasis on the "charismatic leader in mystical contact with the masses" (one of Peter Wiles' characterisations of populism). Even fascist corporatism has distinctly populist attributes. It may be argued that fascism, being racist, should not be confused with populism. Yet Gregor has pointed out that early fascism was in no way racist; this is, above all, a latter-day Nazi aberration. Further, racist themes permeate much of Third World populism; note, for example, the doctrine of Negritude.

Fascism, however, deviates from all populisms in its avowal of the primacy of the Nation-State and its glorification of militarism as an end in itself. Third World populism too is statist, authoritarian and centralist and, to the extent that it can be, often militarist. Yet the Third World populism does not officially espouse the totalitarian presuppositions of fascism: it is always held that any authoritarianism in the regime, or any emphasis on the military organisation, is purely instrumental – a necessary evil for the purposes of the most rapid achievement of the truly popular state to which they profess to aspire. Of course, some populisms are far closer to fascism that others (*cf.* Nkrumah, Poujade, Coughlin).

While fascism is not a species of populism, it has similar sources and it requires only a minimal mutation, as with Marxist-Leninism, for some types of populism to become fascism. And, if populism has similarities to fascism, it also has similarities to anarchism in its distrust of power, of bigness, its stress on decentralism, on the local commune and on consensus. *Populism* is an important summation of the various attributes of a most fascinating social political phenomenon. It is, incidentally, another publication in a first rate series, the Nature of Human Society, published by Weidenfeld.

I would like to close with what I deem a populist-style complaint. Hofstadter's article on North American populism, which is primarily a resumé of relevant parts of his *Age of Reform*, deals only with the Populist Party in the United States. Presumably Canada is part of North America, albeit part of the hinterland, and Canada is, further, the home of two long-lasting widespread populist movement of much more recent vintage, namely the United Farmers Movement and the Social Credit Party.

10.
Peasant Wars of the Twentieth Century

Under the somewhat questionable title *Peasant Wars of the Twentieth Century*,* Eric Wolf, anthropologist at the University of Michigan, broadly describes the background for, and the events of, the revolutions in Mexico, Russia, China, Vietnam, Algeria and Cuba. Even his own descriptions make it difficult to see these revolutions as *peasant* wars. What Wolf is in fact arguing is that in the past peasants initiated rebellions which were localised, self-limiting and invariably successful. In modern times the forces of change, largely seen as the rampages of North Atlantic capitalism, have been so thoroughly disruptive that "when the peasant protagonist lights the torch of rebellion, the edifice of society is already smouldering and ready to take fire". Peasantry then presumably provides the spark and also some of the fuel for the revolution and this is why they are peasant wars. On the other hand, some of the sparks derive from other sources and even if one could tie the truly igniting source to peasantry the point remains that these revolutions, at the moment they become revolutions rather than pure peasant rebellions, are not properly peasant wars. Peasants participate in them in largely abortive rebellion; they provide few leaders and these lose out in the end to non-peasant forces in the revolution (e.g. Zapata, Pancho Villa and Makhno). In other cases (e.g. Cuba and China) peasants are a supportive element of essentially non-peasant political movements. In any event, the further the revolution moves to its culmination, the less the peasants are involved, the more control is vested in an intellectual military elite.

"In all our six cases we witness such a fusion between the 'rootless' intellectuals and their rural supporters", writes Wolf. Certainly peasants do revolt as Wolf says, but would the revolts presumably sparking these six wars have become wars or revolutions if it had not been for the propagandising and organisation of the 'rootless intellectuals' and the involvement of other non-peasants? Might one just as legitimately call these the Wars of the Rootless Intellectuals? Some may choose to call them 'popular' wars, but to call them peasant wars is as misleading

---

* *Peasant Wars of the Twentieth Century* by Eric R. Wolf (Harper & Row, New York, 1969).

as the reference to the Russian Revolution as the proletarian revolution.

Wolf overlooks the irony in the peasant embrace of the Marxist rhetoric, when Marx had nothing but contempt for peasantry and rural life and proclaimed that the highly developed industrial societies were to be the seat of revolution, certainly not under-developed traditional agrarian societies.

Wolf lays the ultimate blame for these major upheavals at capitalism's doorstep. He quotes Bertolt Brecht: "It is not communism that is radical, it is capitalism" by way of suggesting that capitalism under-mined a traditional 'equilibrium' and, while other systems exploited, capitalism alienated as well. This, it seems to me, is an over-simplistic explanation. Obviously capitalism is culpable, yet would it not be more proper to argue that the disruptive elements are a configuration in which capitalism is part of the pattern while the others include a new and enormously efficient technology, a complex industrial organisation and powerful state machine all made more brutally efficient by the most sophisticated bureaucratic techniques. Have the results of the 'peasant' wars in China, Russia or Cuba reduced alienation or exploitation because of the absence of private capitalism? Neo-Marxists overlook the similarities between modern capitalism and modern socialism and so overlook precisely those structural features common to both which produce alienation and exploitation.

While I do not profess to be an authority on each of these wars which Wolf describes, I believe he has composed very readable vignettes and in his concluding chapter proposes challenging generalisations.

ANARCHIST THEORY

11.

Josiah Warren: the incompleat anarchist

Josiah Warren has been presented to the world by his various interpreters as an individualist anarchist and as the first American anarchist. His biographer, W. Bailie, entitled his work *Josiah Warren: The First American Anarchist* (1906). Two recent anthologies of anarchist writings, I.L. Horowitz's *The Anarchists* (1964) and L.I. Krimerman and Lewis Perry's *Patterns of Anarchy* (1966), each have selections from Warren. George Woodcock in his survey of anarchism devotes several paragraphs to Warren and writes: "he developed the theory of the sovereignty of the individual which has led to his being regarded, rightly I think, as the first American anarchist" (1962, 456).

A recent reading of *True Civilization* (1863) and *Practical Details of Equitable Commerce* (1852) has led me to question how far one should classify Warren as an anarchist and to suspect that, certainly as he grew older, he assumed a position like that of Thoreau or even Jefferson which is more accurately described as decentralist democrat and, indeed, seems to form a significant link between various elements of the contemporary radical right (such as the Rampart College group at Larkspur, Colorado) and the anarchist left.

Josiah Warren (1798-1874) was born in New England and, after an early marriage, drifted westward eventually settling in Ohio. By profession an orchestra leader and music teacher, he pursued these enterprises sporadically throughout much of his life. Warren early gave indication of a practical and ingenious turn of mind with his invention of a lard-fed lamp, much cheaper to operate than the usual oil type lamp. Later in his life he turned at different times to produce other inventions. His desire to propagate his social theories led to an interest in printing and the development of a cylinder press which, however, was not accepted by printers until reinvented by another individual a generation later. He also developed a notational system for music and a stereotyping process which brought him $7,000, a sum he invested in his second experimental community of Utopia.

All in all Warren appears to fit the stereotype of the ingenious Yankee tinkering among a variety of gadgets and producing the most practical technological inventions. But Warren was more than a creator of new gadgets. His main claim to fame, of course, is as an innovator and experimenter with social systems. J.S. Mill called Warren "a remarkable American" and it is a sad commentary on the *Encyclopaedia Britannica* and not on Josiah Warren that the encyclopaedia contains not a single reference to so creative and unique an individual.

Martin suggests that, had it not been for his association with Owen, Warren might have devoted the rest of his life to business under-takings and "become one of the early men of wealth in the growing Midwest" (1957, 14). Between 1825 and 1827 Warren was associated with Owen at the New Harmony colony. He saw its major defects as excessive organisation and centralisation and left the community intent upon testing Owen's idea of economic exchange through promissory notes based upon labour time. Like Thoreau, who embarked upon his Walden stay as an experiment, Warren too opened a 'time store' in Cincinnati in 1827 to test the practicality of Owen's labour note theory. After three years of operation Warren closed his store convinced of its feasibility and invited others to join him in founding a community based on what he called the principle of equity, namely that cost of an item was the labour time involved in bringing it to the consumer. Exchange was to be in the form of notes indicating a promise to give on demand so much labour time. In addition the community was to be "based on voluntary assent and lacking the formalities of majority rule" (Martin, 1957, 43). Thus he founded Equity which lasted less than three years and was the shortest lived of his communities. Actually Equity was forced to close not because of the failure of the application of the social theories but because "faulty judgement had resulted in locating the settlement on land in a low-lying area, which subjected the residents to a variety of illnesses. The principal one ... was malaria" (Martin, 1957, 42). Following the Equity experiment Warren variously worked on a new printing press, ran a short-lived manual training school, edited a periodical and operated for two years another time store. In 1847 he established his second community of Utopia and in 1851 still a third called Modern Times. Both were organised according to the same principles as those of Equity and eventually suffered from the ill effects of the Civil War and the availability of cheap lands further west. Both, however, managed to continue on after Warren's death in 1874. Members gradually and quietly abandoned the principles of equity and the communities eventually withered away after a few decades. They had the merit of being the longest lived of any of the secular utopian experiments of the nineteenth century. And this is a point worth bearing in mind, namely that of all the secular experiments of this nature the two which survived the longest were the ones which were the most libertarian.

Warren's views may be broadly described as individualist, rationalist and pragmatic and his earlier writing – for example *Equitable Commerce* – as more specifically anarchist. There is a certain affinity between Warren and Paul Goodman: Warren could well have authored a *Utopian Essays and Practical Proposals*. The central theme of Warren's writings is the 'sovereignty of the individual', by which he meant that the starting place of any philosophy is with the individual who, by implication, is above all a rational being. The primitive condition of man requiring self-preservation produced clan organisation which stressed the supremacy of the group over the individual, the dissolution of individuality in the group, and discouraged all individual responsibility. The clan idea has been perpetuated in modern times in the concept of nationhood, in the 'union of states' and in communism. True civilisation is based on the sovereignty of the individual not of the group.

Before describing the doctrine of self-sovereignty further and its specific relationship to the idea of government – which is the main burden of this paper – it should be pointed out that Warren saw true civilisation as a possibility only when individuality and self-sovereignty operated in concert with what he called the principle of equivalents and the principle of equitable money. The principle of equivalents holds that the price of an item is governed by its cost which in turn amounts to the labour of processing and delivering the item to the consumer. Cost should not be confused with value; to base price on value is an iniquity. One cannot determine value, but one can determine cost by labour exerted. Skill or talent which cost nothing are natural wealth and should be accessible to all without price. Warren, following Owen, advocates the equality of labour: the labour time of the physician is equal to that of the store clerk. This raises the question that if cost of an item varies according to labour time why doesn't the 'cost' of the labour time vary according to the amount of energy and the investment of past training. In other words, should not past preparation and expenditure of energy make the surgeon's hour more costly than the shopkeeper's?

With the principle of equivalents usury disappears and a borrower is charged, as Warren charged his borrowers, for the labour time it takes the lender to arrange for and ultimately collect the loan. The capitalist obtains, under Warren's scheme, only payment for the time invested in overseeing and other similar duties. Warren mentions two factors which will prepare the way for the establishment of this principle. First, stressing the rational nature of man, is the observation that men, capitalist and non-capitalist alike, will see that this approach is most reasonable. Those who do not will, by the operation of 'equitable competition', eventually be forced to engage in 'equitable commerce'. Another essential ingredient of true civilisation is equitable money where notes indicating a promise to provide a stated amount of labour time on demand are used for all commercial transactions. Such a system was applied by Warren in his time stores and in his communities where it apparently met with some success, suffering little from what one might consider its most obvious drawbacks, namely an inability to redeem the notes and depreciation as a result of over-issue.

Warren uses the model of equitable commerce as the basis for his approach to education and all social relations. At one point in his work such economic emphasis is expressed in a naive economic determinism: "Pecuniary affairs are the very basis of society. When we change these we change all institutions, for all are built, directly or indirectly, upon property considerations ... The great excuse for laws and government is the protection of persons and property, but, were it not for property, persons would not be in danger" (*Practical Details*, 71).

When methods of acquiring property are so altered that each may share in an abundance "with less trouble than it will cost him to invade his neighbour" we shall be able to dispense with rules (*Practical Details*, 71). Warren makes, then, in this one instance what today would be considered a vulgar Marxist explanation, but both *Practical Details* and *True Civilization* are permeated with an intellectualistic causal theory intimating that the real dynamic force in society is the rational man who comes to realise his own self-interest.

While Warren continued throughout his life a faith in the principles of equitable commerce, he apparently modified his views concerning

the principles of individuality and self-sovereignty as they relate to the
role of government. Thus Martin writes: "Agitated by the violence
and disruption which was becoming a part of the existence of many
in all parts of the land, Warren published a curious tract, *Modern
Government and its True Mission: a few words for the American crisis*,
which advocates expedients greatly at variance with principles which
have unalterable status among anarchists. A study of the work reveals
a regression to functional aspects long taught by Robert Owen"
(Martin, 82).

Martin does not elaborate further, but when one explores *True
Civilization*, written a year after (in 1863), his meaning becomes more
apparent. Warren here has become the advocate of a form of limited
government much in the tradition of Thomas Jefferson: "The true
function of government deals only with the offensive encroachments
upon persons or property – an expedient choice of evils where there
is nothing but evil to choose from – to prevent unnecessary destruction
of life or property" (*True Civilization*, 28). True civilisation never uses
violence 'unnecessarily' according to Warren. At other places in *True
Civilization* he states: "The Modern Military, as a Government, will
be necessary only in the transitionary stage of society from confusion
and wanton violence to true order and mature civilisation" (33). And
in the concluding pages of the same volume he is apparently not
objecting to government so much as he is opposing 'Aggressive
Government': "And whenever a Government governs an iota more
than is absolutely necessary to restrain or repair unnecessary encroachments on aggression, it then becomes aggressive and should *itself* be
governed and restrained" (179).

Some hints of this interpretation of the role of government appear
in *Practical Details* which Warren published more than ten years before
True Civilization. Thus: "There are some circumstances *under* which
organisation and laws seem to be justifiable which ought to be a
temporary expedient, has been created into a universal rule to which
even the objects aimed at have become subordinate!" (*Practical
Details*, 54). Warren holds this condition is wrong since, again stressing
his pragmatism, he believes each case must be examined on its own.
Later in this short book he discusses his experiences in operating a
manual training school. He presents views on education which are a
nineteenth century pre-visioning of the philosophy of A.S. Neill, as
well as a further application of his practical, libertarian and rationalistic

approach. In brief, he believes children should be motivated to obey not by command, threats or punishment but by the principle of labour for labour, love for love, i.e. the mutualist ideal. Children "have their own sovereignty as much as adults and it should be exercised in the same limits *at their own cost*" (*Practical Details*, 64). On the other hand, and this point is relevant to his remarks on government, "I cannot allow my child to exercise his sovereign will in all things until, in *all* things, he can take the consequences on himself" (68). In other words, I would submit that even in *Practical Details* written by Warren in 1852 there are indications of a trend that finally culminated in *True Civilization* and apparently also in his essay *Modern Government and its True Mission*.

It is interesting to look for a moment at the type of government Warren envisaged. If individuals are unable to settle their affairs by mutual and voluntary contract Warren advocates appeal to deliberative councils composed of members who volunteer their services and are, of course, recognised in their role by the various sovereign individuals. These councils are to act as mediators, but "when an issue has already been raised and no one of these decisions is acceptable to both parties, the decision may be laid before the military (or government) to act at its discretion, selecting that course which promises the least violence" (*True Civilization*, 30).

Warren tends to identify government with the military establishment and hence, in line with his thinking, it is necessary to create a military or 'home guard' composed of sovereign individuals. Thus he suggests that the idea of commanding or governing be replaced by the principle of guidance or direction. "Men may lead and men must execute, but intelligence, principle, must regulate" (*True Civilization*, 22). An essential part of the training of the military is in instilling the idea of individual sovereignty and the protection of the person and property: "Part of the drill for such a force would be to give orders to do some unnecessary harm on purpose to be disobeyed in order to accustom the subordinate to 'look before they leap' or strike!" (*True Civilization*, 27). Such a home guard would be "within but not under discipline" or, in other words, the Sabbath is made for man and not man for the Sabbath.

When the 'counsellors' have referred an issue to this military organisation of sovereign individuals "of course members of the military may themselves assert their inalienable right to decline to act!" (*True*

Civilization, 23). "The most intelligent people always make the best subordinates in a good cause, and in our *modern military* it will require more true manhood to make a good subordinate than it will to be a leader: for the leader may very easily give orders, but they take the responsibility of that *only*, while the subordinate takes the responsibility of executing them, and it will require the greatest and highest degree of manhood, of self-government, presence of mind and real heroism to *discriminate* on the instant and to stand up individually before all the corps and future criticism and assume, alone, the responsibility of dissent or disobedience. His only support and strength would be in his consciousness of being more true to his professed mission than the order was, and in the assurance that he would be sustained by public opinion and sympathy as far as that mission was understood" (23). "When a high degree of intelligence, great manhood, self-government, close discriminating real heroism and gentle humanity are known to be necessary to membership in our military corps (or government), these qualities will come into fashion and become the characteristics of the people; and to be thought destitute of them and unworthy of membership in the military would cause the greatest mortification: while to be known as a member in good standing would be an object sought in the highest honour" (*True Civilization*, 24). If this reasoning is correct Warren believes we have the clue to the "true mission and form of Government – to the most perfect yet harmless subordination – the reconciliation of obedience with FREEDOM – to the cessation of all hostilities between parties and nations – to universal cooperation for universal preservation and security of person and property" (*True Civilization*, 24). Warren's views about the transformation of the military into a body of sovereign and rational individuals appear almost fantastic, particularly in our day when we have been made so much more aware of the nature of military organisation – as the epitome of autocracy and authoritarian structure. Indeed, such ideas appear more the desperate efforts of a man frantically searching for means to salvage his libertarian philosophy in the face of a hitherto harmonious world now shattered by the violence of the Civil War period.

In describing Warren's later views as only peripherally anarchistic I do not wish thereby to imply some doctrinaire definition of anarchism. I conceive of anarchism essentially as being at one end of a pole opposite to absolute despotism or, to put it differently, at one end of a continuum is a condition in which all power is equally diffused among all members of society and at the other end is a condition under which all power is vested in a single person. These are 'ideal types' and it is hardly conceivable that either has ever existed or ever will exist, although certain systems approach one or the other poles and various pressures produce in a social system a dialectic process pushing society in one direction or the other. Obviously Warren's thoughts fit on the anarchistic side of continuum. If Warren was an anarchist in the first half of his life as is evidenced by the nature of his experimental communities, his critique of the Owenite experiments, and by the writings of this period, he had taken towards the close of his life a position which does not appear to fall within that minimal definition of anarchy as the absence of government. Certainly the anarchist society is to be free of the coercive forces of governmental institutions even though numerous other coercive forces will inevitably persist. (And, as some have pointed out, these latter can become more of a threat to individual sovereignty than government.) By placing the military as the ultimate arbiter and permitting individuals within that body to refuse to act, Warren perpetuates authoritarian elements of the present social order and, in addition, enhances the possibilities of 'civil war' between rival factions of the military. Warren, of course, neglected or at least totally underestimated the role of the irrational in man and the effect of cultural forces in moulding men.

Warren was not the only anarchist who did not consistently follow an anarchist position. Proudhon, who in so many ways is similar to Warren and made many keen insights into the nature of government, at various points in his life was elected to the Chamber of Deputies, saw Louis Napoleon as a vehicle for initiating the revolution and sought to legislate a society of free contact. Such difficulties or contradictions as presented by Warren and Proudhon – namely their incisive critiques of government, their plea for freedom and the individual coupled with what is probably best described as a naivete about the essential nature of power, of government and of the military especially – suggest the source of their problem. Neither, I suspect, had the analytic and theoretic turn of mind – more characteristic in a Marx – to dig down to the roots of these institutions and clearly perceive their full implications. Obviously the Civil War disturbance caused Warren to reconsider and reformulate his earlier position. Yet had he more fully comprehended the nature of government and the military, as well as the limits of the rational in man, even in the new light of this crisis, it is difficult to see his reaching the ambiguous and naive conclusions expressed in *True Civilization*.

If anything Warren's and, one can include here as well, Proudhon's struggle to formulate a conception of the free society is only a review of the basic problem facing all libertarians: how can a free society recognise the use of violence as a legitimate technique for resolving issues? Certainly if anarchists are to have an army in their society it would have to be the kind portrayed by Warren but, as I have suggested above, in light of what we know today of human psychology and the nature of the military structure, the possibilities of such an army appear sheer fantasy. The problem in effect comes down to the question can anarchists hold that the threat or use of violence is in any case legitimate? Conversely, can those who call themselves pacifists subscribe to the political theory of the legitimacy of the state?

12.
Law and Anarchism

In 1970 a seminar on anarchism and law was held at Erasmus University in Rotterdam. The present work* is a selection of largely revised papers presented at the seminar. The first two papers are by the editors, Holterman and Van Maarseveen, in turn. They teach constitutional law at Erasmus, while the other authors are all political 'scientists' at either British or American universities.

Almost half of this book is taken up by the Holterman and Van Maarseveen articles. Holterman's 'Anarchist Theory of Law and the State' draws heavily on Kropotkin. Van Maarseveen's article is 'Anarchism and the Theory of Political Law'. Both attempt to reconcile anarchism with legal theory and they are able to do so primarily by confusing and obfuscating terms. Possibly because of their legal training they show us an amazing capability in this regard. Let us consider how they, and in some respects other contributors, have used or abused such concepts as the state, law, arbitration, mediation and decentralisation.

Holterman seeks to redefine the state as "the organisation of relationships which have been characterised as problematic" (14). This, of course, defines about any kind of association whether it be a family, a club or a state. Such vague and general definitions are not just useless, they are a menace, as they contribute to obscurantism and disguise the central significance of such an idea as the state. That central significance which distinguishes the state from any other form of association is that within it the members are divided into a hierarchy of rulers and ruled, and the rulers lay claim to a monopoly on the right to use violence to enforce the laws of the state, or in other words to dominate the ruled.

Surprisingly, while all of the authors comment on the state, the word *government* is not to be found in the entire book. Perhaps Holterman can so redefine government in an equally obscurantist fashion as to be able to say that not only do anarchists believe in a state and law but government as well. After all, anarchists, he says, don't oppose the notion of the state as such, only that of the 'dominant state'.

* *Law and Anarchism* edited by Thom Holterman and Henc Van Maarseveen (Black Rose Books, Montreal, 1984).

Further he comments on his concern to build "an anarchist legal order
in the form of a 'creative democracy'" (45).

A second problem in the book is much more widespread, being
shared not only by the two senior authors but by several others as
well. This is the confusion of the term *law* with *norm* or *custom* in such
a way as to claim that anarchist societies have law. The worst offenders
in this regard are Holterman and Van Maarseveen. Yet Carter, in her
discourse on direct action, claims that whether the ideal anarchist
society will have no law is "clearly disputable". She denies that direct
action necessarily is a display of disrespect for the law. In both cases
she confuses law with custom or moral principle. Throughout her
article on Kropotkin, Cahm repeatedly uses the terms 'customary' or
'popular' law. I believe this is misleading since Kropotkin himself only
rarely employs such terms, but rather uses custom, rules or mutual
aid. Reichert, too, in his article seems to make Proudhon speak of *law*.
While I am not a Proudhon specialist, I do not recall him using the
term as something one would find in a free society.

For any anarchist argument, as well as for any rational understanding of human societies, it is imperative to recognise that there
are on the one hand rules which are imposed by the state through its
government – in other words, laws – and there are other kinds of rules
not imposed by the state but which fall into a category of diffuse and
religious sanctions. Much of the intent of this book seems designed
to destroy this distinction, so critical to anarchist theory.

Perhaps I might briefly clarify further what this distinction entails.
In my book *People Without Government* I pointed out that over a half
a century ago A.R. Radcliffe-Brown suggested that there are three
major kinds of sanctions, referring to negative reactions by a community
to the behaviour of any of its members. Diffuse and religions sanctions
are universal to all human societies, whereas penal sanctions are found
only where there is a state and a government. This is because in penal
sanctions there exist specialised 'enforcers' who lay some claim to
monopolising the uses of violence so as to enforce the rules. Penal
sanctions are therefore laws. Diffuse sanctions lack specialist enforcers.
They may range from such practices as gossip or ostracism, which
may be employed by anyone, to 'organised' sanctions (Radcliffe-
Brown uses this term long before Descallar, author of the final essay
in *Law and Anarchism*). Diffuse sanctions are fundamentally different
from law (penal sanctions) in that in their operation no one claims or

can claim a monopoly on the uses of violence to punish others.

Even in 'organised' sanctions, whoever may act as mediator has behind him only a moral authority or the spontaneous reaction of the community towards an alleged culprit. Religious sanctions may require a human intermediary, such as the specialised power of a priest, so that that person has a special authority not shared with others. Thus this is a kind of religious penal sanction. In contrast, the belief that God strikes me with illness because I profane his name is a direct supernatural sanction not involving the power of any human arbiter and is therefore a different kind of religious sanction, more on the order of an 'act of nature'. Taylor's five types of social control (183-184) are all readily reducible to either religious or diffuse sanctions. An anarchist society is clearly different from a state society in that in it there would be no penal sanctions – no law – while in the state penal sanctions prevail and religious and diffuse sanctions are secondary.

Descallar especially, in 'Anarchism and Legal Rules', confuses arbitration with mediation. This seems to me an especially grave fault when discussing anarchist theory since arbitration would not be found in an anarchist society while mediation would be *the* mechanism for settling disputes. This is because arbitration requires the contesting parties to submit their cases to an arbitrator who has the authority to bring down a decision *that is enforced*. In mediation disputes are settled by a third party who has no authority to see such enforcement of her decisions. They are accepted out of a moral obligation or because the honour of the disputants is at stake or because of the threat of the spontaneous reaction of most or all members of the community, or all of these factors together.

At least one author argues that anarchists themselves ignore the principle of reaching group consensus before a decision is executed and often instead resort to majority vote. However, he does not add that the fundamental difference between anarchist and democratic doctrine in this example is that the minority in the anarchist situation is not compelled by threat of police action to accept the majority decision. In anarchist theory, even if a decision were reached by majority vote, it cannot be forced on the minority. In addition, I think one would find that anarchists would accept decision by majority vote in cases concerning matters of tactics or organisation, but they would be particularly desirous of achieving consensus on issues of basic principle.

Several articles suggest that anarchism is a kind of synonym for decentralisation. Certainly anarchism seeks an equal diffusion of authority in a community among all its members, but decentralising power to smaller groups is not by itself sufficient to establish anarchy. Despotism may occur in a group of ten or ten million.

Now I should like to turn to some of the issues specific to particular articles. Two articles are essentially descriptions of the positions of classical anarchist theoreticians. Cahm states that Kropotkin, like other anarchists, "found it difficult to dissociate the idea of law from the state" (106). For Kropotkin law evolved out of the growing abdication of authority to certain notables who acted as arbiters, enforcing their decisions by reliance upon a warrior band. Kropotkin obviously recognises the importance of shamans and other merchants of thought and knowledge in the evolution of law and state authority, a point later elaborated upon by Arthur Hocart in *Kings and Councillors* (University of Chicago Press, 1970). I do not believe that Kropotkin gives sufficient weight to the role of property and social class in state formation, although he does mention them.

While the evolutionary process entails the gradual predominance of the state, Kropotkin is anxious to preserve some glimmer of hope for mutual aid and regulation by custom which he says still prevails in the village community. The state inhibits mutual aid, but mutual aid and sociability are fundamental traits of humankind which will revive with the return to community.

W.O. Reichert, in discussing Proudhon, perhaps relies too heavily on secondary sources rather than going directly to the works of Proudhon himself. Proudhon, like Marx, altered his views in the course of his writing career and this I think deserves more attention, both by Reichert and Holterman.

For example, in *What is Property?* and *The General Idea of the Revolution in the Nineteenth Century*, Proudhon takes a clear anarchist position, but in *Du Princip Federatif* he advocates a weak or minimal central government.

Reichert notes that the basis for Proudhon's social philosophy is in the concept of justice which Proudhon identifies with voluntary association through reciprocity. Distributive justice, the notion that a third-party authority figure must regulate the distribution of goods, must be replaced by commutative justice which establishes the sovereignty of the individual, voluntary contract and reciprocity.

Proudhon, says Reichert, advocates a theory of laissez faire: humans are social as well as economic beings. People "therefore have the capacity of settling their differences equitably without help from outside" (132).

In his concluding remarks Reichert observes that "individuals may deprive other individuals of favours or otherwise seek to compel them to do or not do something, but so long as they do not hold a monopoly over the goods of society, genuine coercion can hardly be said to exist" (138). He then quotes Hayek on the conditions under which 'true coercion' occurs. But completely overlooked is the very genuine and 'real' coercive force of the controllers and manipulators of ideas – the shamans, the priests, the intellectuals.

Carter focuses on direct action and its relevance to anarchism. Central to her article is the question of the relevance to anarchism of direct action aimed at changing laws. Here is raised the old question for radicals as to what extent one should compromise with the world and seek short-term 'liberalising' improvements. Carter comes down definitely on the side of the compromisers.

I think anarchists will find Taylor's article 'Social Order Without the State' the best in this collection. Among other things it has the merit of not becoming mired in terminological confusion. His article summarises much of the material in his *Anarchy and Cooperation* and *Community, Anarchy and Liberty*. He first argues that social order is a "public good" and then criticises liberal arguments for the state. He notes that even if "we suppose that large publics will not voluntarily provide themselves with public goods – it does not follow that the state is the *only* means of ensuring the supply of such goods or that other means would not suffice and must be supplemented by the state" (167). Also, the liberal argument that people are too egotistic to want to contribute to the public good is criticised by Taylor on the ground that the lack of altruism in people may well be the product of long-standing state intervention.

For me, one of the strongest arguments favouring the existence of the state is that the state arises in a situation where there is an enormous increase in complexity of the division of labour such that very many specialisations and special interests occur. This produces extremes of heterogeneity where little or no common interests, values or beliefs exist among groups who are flung together in daily social intercourse. Thus to impose some minimum of commonality and social control the state/government is established. This argument also has significance as an explanation for the origin of the various 'world' religions which may be said to appear so as to provide a common ground for an otherwise highly diverse population. Perhaps Taylor might have addressed this point of view. He would no doubt observe that this view still does not explain why it is only state organisation which should arise and why some alternative forms of organisation might not be equally capable of producing order. Yet I wonder if Taylor in his conclusion, and in a sort of backhanded way, does not give support to this argument for the state when he says that anarchy is not possible without community and that the first requirement of community is *common beliefs and values*. I agree with Taylor, but it seems that all of this points to what may well be insurmountable problems. On a more positive note, I would observe that recent years have seen a kind of convergence between anarchist theory and anthropological theory, especially where anthropologists have come to place greater emphasis upon the role of reciprocity, mutual aid and co-operation in the genesis and development of human society. And, of course, anthropologists have pointed, often times unwittingly, to those many viable alternatives to state organisation.

In sum, after reading this book I think it must be reaffirmed that anarchy is liberty and order without the state, government, law or democracy – 'creative' or otherwise. Any attempt to suggest differently, as is too frequently the case in this book, is an attempt to dissolve, yes, destroy the very core of anarchist society.

13.
Pierre-Joseph Proudhon

As near as I can determine there have been in the last thirty years six major studies in the English language on Proudhon, which is more than all that have gone before. This may not exactly demonstrate a recent surge of interest, yet it indicates that Proudhon is more widely recognised in English-speaking intellectual circles today than in the period from his death in 1865 to 1956. Perhaps this is related to the parallel increased concern for decentralisation, anti-modernism and anti- or non-Marxist forms of socialism.

K. Steven Vincent's book *Pierre-Joseph Proudhon and the Rise of French Republican Socialism*,* which is a version of his PhD dissertation, places Proudhon in the social historical context of his time showing the influences which impinged upon him. Important here are Montesquieu and Rousseau among other, mostly French, theoreticians. Vincent does also what many in intellectual history tend to ignore. Namely, he shows how the practical organisation of ordinary working men contributed to the formulation of social theory. In this case the Lyon woollen weavers' associations are seen as instrumental in the evolution of Proudhon's mutualism. Many biographies lead us to believe that the ideas of the great man are an original product of great genius thrust into the world full blown. This is avoided with the present biography. Not only is Proudhon placed within the context of the milieu of nineteenth century French republican socialism and its intellectual currents, but one can better appreciate the continuities and parallels between Proudhon and later French thought in Durkheim, Mauss and Levi-Strauss.

The book follows Proudhon on an intellectual journey demonstrating the gradual evolution and change in his ideas. Indeed the change in his ideas over time underlines the necessity for a chronological approach to the understanding of any man's thoughts. Vincent considers that from 1832 to 1842 Proudhon can be called a Christian socialist. He soon came to reject the Roman Catholic Church but he did not reject Jesus or God. Eventually Proudhon

---

* *Pierre-Joseph Proudhon and the Rise of French Republican Socialism* by K. Steven Vincent (Oxford University Press, New York, 1984).

evolved what Vincent calls mutualist socialism and finally, in the last
half-decade of his life, federalism. Proudhon only gradually adopted
an anarchist position. Until 1846, or 1849 at the latest, he believed
his mutualist socialism would be instituted with the aid of the
government. And at no time did he believe that anarchy could develop
overnight. While it would eventually triumph, it would only evolve
slowly. In the meantime he supported various short-term approaches
or 'immediate demands', that is political tactics which may seem
highly irregular to most anarchists. He ran for public office, served as
a member of the French National Assembly, supported Louis Napoleon
(because he thought the alternative monarchists posed a major threat
– much as Lyndon Johnson attracted so much support in 1964
because of the greater fear of Barry Goldwater). Proudhon wrote
programmes which advocated compulsory military service and a
national assembly organised on a corporatist basis. Unlike Godwin,
Proudhon had doubts about the essential goodness of human beings,
believing our species was weak and readily tempted by evil. We may
note further that throughout his life Proudhon was a strong believer
in the traditional family and in the subordination of women. At the
same time he denounced centralised authority and called himself an
anarchist.

This all suggests a common observation about Proudhon: that he
was a paradoxical and contradictory individual. In some respects
Proudhon is made less contradictory if we take up his ideas in proper
chronological order and remember that he did change his mind now
and then. Another problem was Proudhon's tendency to make
exaggerated and sometimes wild statements which he really did not
mean, or to use terms in a very idiosyncratic fashion. His well-known
statement that property is theft is a case in point. In actual fact
Proudhon was a dedicated believer in property, but property in the
sense of materials which could be used by the owner, but not that
property which could be used to extract what Marxists call surplus
value.

George Woodcock tried to explain the contradictions in Proudhon
by pointing to his peasant background, although I do not believe he
explicates this issue adequately. The point is that if we look at the
nineteenth century French peasant we may often find such
Proudhonian values emphasising the patriarchal family, local and
regional autonomy, small face-to-face groups, reciprocity, consensus-

style politics. Hard work and frugality are stressed as well as morality and pragmatism. To account for Proudhon's paradoxical thoughts Vincent stresses the pragmatic. Proudhon believed one had to make practical choices between bad alternatives and so, as a political tactic, would sometimes endorse candidates for public office or even run himself.

With all his hatred of authority and love of liberty Proudhon seems essentially naive about the insidious ways of power. In this Proudhon comes very close to Marx. At least at some periods in his life he seems to have believed the state could be used to destroy itself. At the end of his life, however, Proudhon, now a rather embittered person, advocated withdrawal from the world so as to set up a new society and demonstrate to the world the merits of anarchism.

As an intellectual biography Vincent's correctly stresses descriptions and analyses of Proudhon's major writings. For his early and formative years the author does not rely on primary sources but almost exclusively upon Pierre Haubtmann, a Catholic writer. It is, incidentally, both interesting and odd that two Catholic writers (Haubtmann and DuLubac) should produce major studies of Proudhon, the anti-theist and anti-papist. Vincent devotes less than ten percent of his book to the last four or five years of Proudhon's life, years characterised by a high degree of productivity. Oddly enough there is not a word about his death; Proudhon just fades away. Moreover nothing is said about Proudhon's wife, his marriage or his children – subjects which are not irrelevant to an intellectual biography, especially to one such as Proudhon who was a devoted family man.

If biographers of Proudhon like Woodcock and Hyams tend to over-emphasise Proudhon's anarchism, Vincent clearly down-plays it. In discussing the *Idée générale de la révolution au XIXe siècle* and *Du principe fédératif*, I do not believe he brings out sufficiently the anarchist sentiment expressed in these works. At the same time he is at pains to point up the clearly non-anarchist views of Proudhon. He presents in some detail Proudhon's programme of 1848 favouring a corporate state. Strangely enough he does not note its relationship to fascist corporatism of the twentieth century. Woodcock too briefly refers to this programme but he only notes Proudhon's advocacy of compulsory military training. Hyams and Hoffman totally ignore the programme.

Vincent devotes quite a bit of space to Proudhon's first work, *De la célébration du Dimanche*, but argues that the title is misleading. He contends it is a very important book because Proudhon here lays out all the major political themes to which he devoted the rest of his life. Several of Proudhon's significant studies are never discussed at all by Vincent. Certainly in a work of this nature there is no excuse for totally ignoring the enigmatic and highly controversial *La guerre et la paix*.

Proudhon was obviously a many-faceted and extremely complex individual who held to many notions which today would be unacceptable for most anarchists. Aside from what has already been noted it should also be pointed out that Proudhon, like his contemporaries, worshipped at the altar of automatic progress and modern science. Moreover, he had a naive idea of what science is. But there is no doubt that he was a most original thinker who made major contributions to anarchism in his critique of government and his programme of mutualism and federalism. Additionally, he played an important role in developing such ideas as the commodity dollar, the credit union and the social credit doctrine.

Unlike Marx, Engels, Lenin and all the other bourgeois socialists, Proudhon was born of peasant stock and spent the greater part of his life as a member of the working class. He knew what it was to be a worker. A prodigious writer, in the course of 25 years he wrote over twenty book-length works in addition to numerous articles. Of course many of them do read as if they were merely written off the top of the head. The nature of the modern publishing business is such that if Proudhon had lived today most of his works would probably only have seen the light of day through some vanity press.

Despite the criticisms of Proudhon, I am enough of a peasant, anti-modernist and neolithic conservative – to use Paul Goodman's term – to consider Proudhon one of my favourite social philosophers. Vincent's study should be read along with those of Woodcock, Hyams and Hoffman, for they complement one another – that is, if you can afford the price.

14.
Anarchism and Cities

In his *Freedom* article 'Anarchism and Cities', [16th November 1991] Jonathan Simcock has, I believe, overlooked a most crucial factor, namely the heterogeneity of cities and the problem this presents to the anarchist. In all past anarchic polities urban life has been an extremely rare phenomenon. Indeed, it seems that it has only been found in connection with the brief attempts at establishing anarchist societies by Makhno in the Ukraine and by the Spaniards in the 1936-39 period. While many anarchic people such as the Ifugao and the Tonga did evolve complex social relations, they did not have cities. In my view the maintenance of city life poses a real challenge to any anarchic system. This is because, on the one hand, cities are inherently heterogeneous in their composition and, on the other hand, anarchy appears most successful in situations where participants live in small face-to-face homogeneous groups. That is, the anarchist experiment seems to work best where individuals are well acquainted with one another, and are most likely kinsmen, and where they share most of their beliefs, customs and other habits. This in a way contradicts the usual anarchist propensity for variety and emphasis on individuality, but the point is, to be brief, sameness and homogeneity make social peace easier to maintain.

The city since its inception has been characterised above all by a specialised division of labour. Such specialisation entails a differentiation from those who do not share one's speciality. Butchers, bakers and candlestick makers each develop their own unique concerns, interests and language so that they have less in common, less mutual understanding and less agreement with one another. In addition, cities from their inception attracted all kinds of people from a great variety of cultural and sub-cultural backgrounds. They have drawn people from the several regions of the rural 'outback' and people from divergent religious and other belief systems. Consequently, in contrast to the rural village, we know the city as a place where an immense variety of individuals dwell. Such variety readily provokes conflicting views and interests. While the rural village also has its conflicts – and all human groups do – it avoids the very basic kinds of conflict engendered by the urban context where people living cheek by jowl have little in common with each other. In the rural village there is little or no specialisation of labour. Members share in the rules of the game, the values, beliefs and rituals of the community.

A central problem of the city, then, has been how to accommodate the variety of life dwelling within it so that at least there will be peace among groups. In other words, how do you maintain order in a highly heterogeneous social milieu?

Humans have employed primarily three techniques to deal with this problem: the state, the 'world' or 'universal' religion, and the ghetto. One of the strongest arguments justifying the existence of the state has been that it is an institution which presumably is established to integrate a highly diverse society and to arbitrate the inevitable difference and conflicts which arise in such societies. It is no coincidence that historically the city, social class and the state appear at the same time and in the same places. Out of the diverse elements which compose a city, a dominant elite arises to act as the chief arbitrator. It not only arises because it has more power, but also because those outside that elite acquiesce in the belief that they will have personal security. As de la Boetie long ago pointed out, the mass of people may be readily 'conned' into what amounts to selling their freedom for some alleged security.

The adoption of a 'universal' or 'world' religion is another technique for attempting to provide bonds which will unite an otherwise divided population. Confucianism, Taoism, Buddhism, Hinduism, Judaism and Zoroastrianism all arose in the first millennium BCE. Christianity appeared at the beginning of our era and Islam in the seventh century. And they all arose in urban contexts. Again, these are not mere coincidences. If, for example, a Greek-speaking physician had nothing else in common with another resident of the city who was an Aramaic-speaking water carrier, he might at least share the same Christian religion. The rulers of the Roman Empire sought to impose a minimal unity in their highly heterogeneous domain by requiring that everyone pay obeisance to Ceasar. Shinto arose and spread in Japan, also, in part as an attempt to provide national integration and solidarity in an urbanising heterogeneous society. Of course, we note in passing that each religion became a secondary technique subordinate to the state for each became a tool for reinforcing state authority.

Finally, archaic cities and, still today, some African and Asian cities are divided into quarters or ghettos. The inhabitants of the quarter ordinarily share a common religious, ethnic and linguistic milieu and often these are associated as well with a common occupation or cluster of occupations. Here again, a major intent of such an arrangement is to inhibit inter-group conflict. Each quarter is a more homogeneous, village-like community, the inhabitants of which share common customs and outlook and interact primarily with their own kind. Contact with outsiders is minimised and relations between different groups are regulated by the dominant elite through the overriding state and religious institutions.

Now, how would anarchists address the problem of maintaining social peace in a densely populated, highly heterogeneous city environment? I certainly do not have any blueprint, but would make a few suggestions that are of a very general nature. First, a firm education in a broad set of beliefs would be fundamental and imperative. In other words, there would at a minimum be a necessity to share a body of ethical beliefs – to adopt some (secularised?) modified form of the 'universal' religion idea, including the general ethical core found in all these religions. This ethical core, of course, includes the so-called golden rule and the generation of a respect for others. Any review of previous anarchic societies indicates that self-control and restraint are immensely important. There must be the development of an intense sense of social responsibility and of 'maturity' and the abandonment of 'childish' ways. Each should be taught to act as he pleases so far as it does not interfere with others. (I vaguely recollect that some months ago a correspondent in *Freedom* pooh poohed this idea, arguing that one should consequently not act so as to interfere with, say, the banker's freedom to exploit others. But that is a silly misreading of this prescription. If the banker abided by the rule, as he should, he would not exploit others.) Other ideological systems have never been very successful at inculcating these ideas and I suppose there is no reason to believe anarchists could do any better or even as well, yet for anarchy to work anywhere, and especially in the urban environment, it seems to me these ideas have to be indelibly imprinted on the consciences (super-egos) of all.

In addition to the above, I would suggest that an adequate mediation system to which individuals feel morally obliged to adhere would be imperative. (Mediation is different from arbitration in that the mediator cannot enforce his decision with the threat of violence or force.) And I think something of a social order based on a network system would be important. I outlined examples of this kind of arrangement in an article in *The Raven* (No. 7, July 1989), 'Segmental Acephalous Network Systems'. Very briefly, this entails every person being a member of a number of different groups, which in turn are a part of a network of further obligations so that any negative action against an individual or group resulting from one set of relations has its counter-restraining effect resulting from affiliation with other groups and individuals. This fine mesh of counter-balancing segments serves to integrate and give order to society.

List of Sources

Chapter 1: 'Culture: the Unifying Concept of Anthropology' in *Culture: the Human Way* (1986, pp.17-42).

Chapter 2: 'The Dynamics of Culture' in *Culture: the Human Way* (1986, pp. 77-123).

Chapter 3: 'Do Anarchic Polities have a Message' in *People Without Government: an Anthropology of Anarchy* (1982 and 1990, pp.121-150).

Chapter 4: Review of Pierre Clastres, *Society Against the State*, in *Our Generation*, Vol. xiv, 1980.

Chapter 7: 'The Renewal of the Quest for Utopia' in *Canadian Confrontations*, edited by A.K. Davis (1970, pp. 60-65).

Chapter 8: 'Argenta, British Columbia: an Experiment in Community' in *Alternative Values and Structures*, edited by S.S. Sandhu (1973, pp. 32-36).

Chapter 9: Review of G. Ionescu and Ernest Gellner (editors), *Populism: Its Meaning and Natural Characteristics*, in *Journal of Human Relations*, Vol. xix, 1971.

Chapter 10: Review of Eric Wolf, *Peasant Wars of the Twentieth Century*, in *Journal of Human Relations*, Vol. xix, 1971.

Chapter 11: 'Josiah Warren: the Incompleat Anarchist' in *Anarchy*, No. 85, 1968 (pp.90-96).

Chapter 12: Review of Thomas Holterman and Henc Van Maarseveen (editors), *Law and Anarchism*, in *Journal of Social Anarchism*, 1986.

Chapter 13: Review of K.S. Vincent, *Pierre-Joseph Proudhon and the Rise of French Republican Socialism*, in *Journal of Social Anarchism*, 1987.

Chapter 14: 'Anarchism and Cities' in *Freedom*, 25th January 1992 (p. 8).

The Raven
ISSN 0951 4066

Harold Barclay has contributed these articles to our 96-page quarterly journal The Raven

---

No 7 (1989)   'Segmental Acephalous Network Systems: alternatives to centralised bureaucracy'

No. 9 (1990)   'Male/Female Relations and the Anthropological Record'

No.18 (1992)   'Anthropology and Anarchism'

No 19 (1992)   'Mutual Aid and Conflict Resolution in the Traditional Egyptian Village'

No. 27 (1994)   'The Roman Catholic Church: the lamb, the fox and the tiger in one unholy trinity'
'Protestant Tradition, Moral Majority and Freedom'

No. 30 (1995)   'Comment on John Zerzan's Critique of Agriculture'

All back issues of The Raven are available at £3.00 each
(post-free worldwide)

Subscriptions for four issues:
Inland £12 / Institutions £18
Abroad: Surface £14; Airmail (Europe) £16; Airmail (rest of
world) £18 / Institutions Surface £22; Airmail £27

Payment with order please. Cheques in Sterling payable to
Freedom Press (payment in US Dollars payable to Chips
Booksearch)
Giro account 58 294 6905

Freedom Press, 84b Whitechapel High Street, London E1 7QX